Escaping Wealth's Waiting Room

Why Timeless Laws Shape Wealth Creation.
Why Everyone Holds Wealth's Seed.
How Every Choice Determines Your Harvest.

Niyi J. Faldo

Copyright

Acknowledgment

To the Divine Architect of stories, the Source before the stream, whose breath turns clay into living soul and whose voice calls order out of chaos, I bow in gratitude. Every insight, every line, every truth that leaps from these pages is but the echo of Your voice in my spirit. You whispered revelation; I merely gave it ink. Without You, there would be no message, no manuscript, no me.

To my beloved family, my greatest treasure on earth, thank you for being my steady place, my well of laughter, and my daily reminder of God's goodness. To my disciple-maker, your whispers became the rhythm of my pen; your voice runs through every chapter. May these words justify the doors you opened. To the teachers who sharpened me like iron against iron, to my covenant circle and friends, whose wisdom shaped my thinking and whose faith sharpened my courage, you have been pillars in the storm and steady hands that lifted me when the weight of the vision pressed hard. Your prayers were wind beneath these words; and the oil that kept the lamp burning. I honour your deposit in my life.

To my tribe: the believers at Potter's House, NCC, CAC, and the many conferences and fellowships where I've had the privilege of sharing some of these principles, you fed me with faith and refused to let me shrink my voice. You are part of the scaffolding God used to build this work. To the midnight warriors who read drafts by dim light and said "dig deeper." You know who you are, this story is our shared altar.

To every heart that will hold these pages, you are not holding mere pages but a prophetic instrument. You are handling a seed with the power to change your seasons. You are why I wrote with my veins open. These are not mere principles; they are spiritual currents, carrying those who obey them into realms of increase. Read them as a seed, not a souvenir. You are reading destiny, and destiny, in turn, is reading you. May these words meet you exactly where you need them, like a letter slipped into your hands at the perfect moment.

This book is no full stop, it is a covenant. It stands as a living promise that truth still roars like thunder, and that a word, spoken in its appointed time, can open the skies.

The Author : Niyi Faldo 08/08/25

Dedication

The dedication of this book is split three ways:

To Theresa,
who first stirred these truths in the silence of my youth.

To Rebecca,
who lived these principles with quiet grace.

And to you, Patience, my enduring flame,
who walked this path with me, through shadows and storms,
when the tide conspired to turn us back.

Foreword

I have known the author for over three decades, an insightful teacher, meticulous to the finest detail, steadfast in truth, and unwavering in purpose. So it comes as no surprise that *Escaping Wealth's Waiting Room* is both profound and practical. Yet, even with my long acquaintance, I found myself awestruck at the deep wells of wisdom poured into this piece. Each page springs with depth that illuminates the path to wealth creation, offering not mere theory but a transformative roadmap for the journey to financial prosperity.

This is not just another book on personal finance. No, it is a divinely inspired map, drawn from ancient truths that have stood the test of time. Here, ancient biblical principles bloom into practical reality. Here, the author skilfully uncovers the wealth-building principles embedded in Scripture, not as lofty theories, but as real, tangible truths you can live by. These are treasures hidden in plain sight, passages we've quoted before, even preached from, without truly understanding their true power to guide us into reshaping our financial destiny.

What makes this work exceptional is not its elegance alone, but its authenticity. The author doesn't peddle common clichés or recycled rhetoric. Instead, he brings tested, Scripture-backed truth, lessons forged in the fire of experience, victories born out of challenges, and testimonies that inspire transformation.

As I read, I recognised the financial missteps I had made, choices that led to years of struggle and debt. Yet within these pages, I found clarity; I found hope; I found a way out. Practical steps, spiritual truths, and timely wisdom merged onto a path I've now begun to walk, and the fruit is undeniable.

To you, dear reader, I offer a heartfelt challenge.
Approach this book not as a casual reader, but as a seeker.
Be ready to learn, to unlearn, and to relearn. Be willing to pause, reflect, and then act. True transformation demands action. Let these insights catalyse immediate changes in how you steward your resources.

Ask yourself: What do I do with the income I receive daily, weekly, monthly? Do I consume what should be invested? Do I scatter my seed on fruitful fields, or barren soil? Have I truly honoured God with what He has placed in my hands?

Escaping Wealth's Waiting Room answers these questions, and many more, with crystalline clarity. It invites you on a journey of financial awakening, spiritual enlightenment, and purposeful action.

I wholeheartedly recommend this book to everyone who dares to break free from the cycles of lack and step into a life of stewardship, multiplication, and divine prosperity.

Stephen Olat.

Table of Contents

Introduction 11

1. The Brutal Laws of Growing True Riches 20
2. The Non-Negotiable Law of Seed and Bread 37
3. The No-Nonsense Law of Seedtime and Harvest 45
4. The Uncompromising Law of Value Exchange 57
5. The Mirage of "Miracle Money" 71
6. God's Funnels of Provision... 97
7. Man's Funnel of Receiving 118
8. Seed-Bread Ratio 141
9. The King's Portion 149
10. The Seed for Your Field: Your Escape Route.................. 202
11. All Seeds Are not equal 225
12. Roaming the Crowded Lane to Poverty 267
13. Switching Lane to Wealth Creation Bypass 285
14. ncremental Power of Sown Seed................................. 337

Introduction

To every soul who labours with trembling faith, to those who plant seeds with bleeding fingers, who trust the invisible arithmetic of sacrifice, who bend their knees with the scars of a thousand deferred promises. To the professionals grinding in silent exhaustion, the parents stretching love like a fraying rope, the dreamers whose hope hums louder than laughter. To the Christian whose tithe and offering disappear into the abyss, and still, you reach deeper into your ribs to give again, only to watch the earth swallow it all without a receipt.

I write.

The "prophetic gate" has refused to open. The drought at home hasn't lifted either. Instead, the silence has grown thicker. And slowly, desperation has now wrapped itself in worship robes around your finances. You have prayed. You have confessed in faith. But the financial crisis is often getting worse, occasionally getting out of hand. They are almost drowning you, and your faithful soul is fainting already.

Debt told you to quit already. The devil swore your obedience was all wasted.

What if I told you poverty doesn't tremble at your tithe? That giving offering, by itself, is no magic wand in creating kingdom riches and wealth? That prayer by men of hefty anointing doesn't re-route riches in your direction? What if all you've been doing is playing your heart out to the wrong jingle, earnest, but misdirected?

The Kingdom of God is not built on ignorance dressed in worship. It thrives in light. And when light shows up, even well-meaning error must retreat. You have been a generous giver at church. But God is not mocked by our ignorance nor moved by an emotional generosity that ignores His protocols. The world keeps ledgers, but heaven remembers the weight of principles. And heaven's economy does not bend to emotional blackmail. It responds to laws.

We are a generation that has sung its way into poverty, danced through debt, and shouted hallelujah over systematic scarcity. But heaven has never been moved by motion. It moves by alignment: alignment with laws, with seasons, with wisdom.

You've prayed long. You've fasted hard. You've poured oil into empty wallets.

Now, read.

Your tears are not lost, they are as liquid fire in the vials of the Almighty. Your silence is not surrender; it's the gathering force of a hurricane in the spirit. That bread you gave from your last meal? It'll one day be worth a five-course feast of kings. That seed you planted in the storm? It's able to penetrate the earth with resurgent force.

The Mighty One rides upon the whirlwind. The Holy One has not forgotten. Every drop of sweat is as a diamond in His vault. He counts. He remembers. And His sickle is thirsty for your harvest.

I know you're never lazy. I know you're putting in your best. You're possibly ill-informed or misinformed. And in the absence of truth, zeal becomes a trap.

On these pages, I do not intend to whisper to your emotions, but call your mind to rise. I do not mean to mock your tears either. I prefer to honour them but refuse to let them flow for long so that they don't drown your discernment.

There are two roads illustrated in this book. Both are paved with intentions, but intentions don't decide destinations, principles and actions do. One road roars with applause, glitters with zeal, and echoes with the noise of well-wishers. Many believers walk it with steam. It is crowded. It is celebrated. But it is hollow. Beneath its pageantry, poverty takes root, subtle, disguised, but growing still. This road leads straight to hardly enough en route aggravated poverty.

The other road is less-travelled, quiet, and less theatrical. But it is lined with wisdom. Those who find it uncover treasures that do not wither and riches that remember the covenant. Both roads wear familiar signs, but only one is lit with the understanding of what simplifies and expedites the sprout of prosperity. The other, often a theatre of activity, is the pathway where poverty buds and blooms but hides in plain sight.

Everyone is unavoidably a voyager on either of these two roads. Every soul is already walking, either toward financial bloom or en route economic barrenness. The roads are not chosen by chance, but by choice. Their driveways exemplify the principles from which the root of generational poverty blooms and upon which the shoot of enduring prosperity blossoms. One path waters the root of divine prosperity, anchored in understanding, fertilized by obedience, and crowned with fruits that endure. The other path, though paved with activity, breeds the branches of lack, predictable, repeatable, and devastatingly avoidable. Your actions are not just habits; they are seeds. And your decision is not just a lifestyle; it is prophecy in motion.

This is the painful truth: many churchgoers are not poor because they don't give. They are poor because they give wrongly, repeatedly, when they should be building. They give emotionally where they should be investing intelligently. They've been taught erroneously to "move God" with money, but have never been taught how to move themselves with skill and strategic investment. So, they confuse sacrificial offerings with a sustainable strategy.

Yet, the truth remains: God honours sowers who understand and align with seasons, not spenders seeking shortcuts. And until your seed starts producing value, not just tears, nothing will shift, not in your bank account, not in your legacy.

You cannot trade divine principles for human hype. You cannot bypass the byway of financial wisdom and expect to arrive at abundance. Heaven's wealth is not accessed through sentiment; it's unlocked through alignment. And alignment demands that you surrender your mind before your money, your effort before your emotions, your value before your vow. You may be up and doing in community and fellowship duties and even have some doors of spiritual blessings widely opened to you, but those things don't reduce your drought or change your financial fortune if you do not comply with the laws that govern kingdom prosperity.

This book is a holy confrontation. It's a defibrillator to shock slumbering minds awake. It's a surgical hand pulling back the veil that religion draped over responsibility. It's not written as a rebuke; but as a jarring light in the tunnel where you've been told to just "pray through" and experience your breakthrough. It holds your hand, not to shout louder but to see clearer; not to just pray through but to also walk through.

This book won't sprinkle fairy dust on your finances. But it will hand you a compass: not of shortcuts, but of sure codes. It doesn't promise a financial miracle overnight. But it offers you the truths that move mountains in due course. It will show you the sure currency that builds abundance and sustains wealth creation. It will show you that making, managing, multiplying, and mastering money are forms of stewardship, far more enduring than all-night "prophetic money" crusades.

Your decision is a choice. Your indecision is also a choice. The former liberates from the shackles of poverty, but the latter confines with fetters of hardly enough. The scriptural protocols highlighted herein never intended to make any kingdom citizen poor. Rather, they serve everyone with outcomes directly proportional to the choices they make and the actions they take in this mandatory voyage where doses of wealth and poverty are routinely distributed without bias.

As you choose your escape route; your lane produces its intended outcome. If you choose the overcrowded-lane on the road to lack and enduring legacies of poverty, no amount of church activities and hefty anointing can change the outcome of your choice. It is only if you change your track that you get the chance to change your outcome. And if you decide on the byway to superabundance and financial freedom, you may experience months or few years of delay because of the initial congestion at the first few miles of the escape route and some strict traffic rules along the journey, but this lane does not deny voyagers of its obligations.

You may have inherited a path of scarcity passed down like an old coat from parents and grandparents. But that coat can be shed. That road can be exited. You can chart a fresh path, not just for yourself but for generations after you. The highway to poverty is paved with good intentions and poor execution, but the byway to enduring riches is marked by hard truth, wise steps, and brave shifts. Your choice determines whether you will end up a decisive partaker of kingdom riches or a wishful onlooker.

The choice is no longer between riches and poverty. It's between truth and tradition; between real wealth and religious wishing, between faith with wisdom and faith wrapped in fantasy.

This isn't a prosperity gospel. It's a roadmap for growing kingdom riches. This is not a magic formula; it's a mirror that reflects predictable financial outputs based on your input. And maybe, just maybe, after all the night watches and sacrificial giving, what you need most is not another seed to sow, but a new lens to see.

The guidelines for traveling on these two roads are inflexible. They unfold principles assured to open up whoever follows through to a life of riches and abundance, yet verified to condemn anyone who ignores them into certain degrees of wants and inadequacies in the medium term, and alleviated or aggravated poverty down the pike. Each route has predictable outcomes.

These pages will guide you to challenge routine barriers, embrace personal lifestyle changes, and address the exact root causes of barely enough and aggravated poverty, whether individualized or multigenerational. You will learn to reshape the common backgrounds of 'from salary to spending' and 'from income to expenditure'; and employ financial principles to create pathways to thrive and prosper. You will encounter both the vision and the tools to transmute your single income stream into flowing rivers of abundance.

If you are ready to learn, unlearn, relearn, and follow these financial codes and culture, you can transform your life through time-tested financial wisdom and intelligence, and switch roads from barely-enough to super-abundance.

Solemn Invitation

Poverty isn't polite. Debt isn't well-mannered either. Principles don't care about your comfort. It's either you plant or perish. The laws highlighted on these pages don't negotiate.

Here is your invitation to transform leaden thoughts into pure gold of financial wisdom. Through the mists of uncertainty, a fresh path can emerge: one where every decision becomes a brushstroke on the graphics of your future wealth, every lesson a key unlocking doors to prosperity. Here, in the intersection of knowledge, wisdom, and intelligence, you, too, can take part in the esteemed dance of kingdom wealth creation, a melody that can echo through generations and turn yesterday's whispers of scarcity into tomorrow's songs of abundance.

Here is your invitation to unleash the transformative power of financial intelligence, break the cycle of poverty and usher in a brighter, more fulfilling future for you and your family line. Here is your invitation to break even the thickest chains of scarcity and transform them into wings of opportunity. Here is your invitation to dance with possibility, weave fresh stories of kingdom riches, and craft a legacy that flows like a mighty river through generations.

Welcome on board. The door of wealth's waiting room is wide open. It's time to pull up poverty by its roots and tap directly into the wellspring of enduring prosperity.

Chapter 1

The Brutal Laws of Growing True Riches

Myth Waylays, but Truth Liberates

Deck or garnish it all you can; you do not do God any favour if you live and die a poor Christian! Tone or tint it as much as possible; you do not deplete God's resources if you walk in kingdom abundance. Poverty, whether softened or severe, does not make you a better Christian. And prosperity, whether worked for or handed down, doesn't stain your salvation either. You're not more sanctified because you struggle, and you're not less redeemed because you thrive. The blood of Jesus is not diluted by the deposit or withdrawal column of your bank statement.

Poverty is not a medal for godliness, and prosperity is not contempt of the gospel. More often, lack lingers where light is lacking, whether it's because truth is distorted or obedience is absent. Sometimes, it's a combination of partial understanding, half-hearted application, and a touch of wanting to take shortcuts with God. Kingdom wealth flows from clarity of truth, alignment with divine patterns, and repeated obedience that matches authentic revelation. Do you desire kingdom abundance? There are habitual choices to make. There are consistent actions to repeat. There are biblical principles to follow.

Talking about biblical principles, I am not referring to those lopsided propositions of breakthrough offering, uncommon giving, seed-faith schemes, painful giving, or any such emotional tactics many are told to employ in order to attract God's attention and 'provoke' Him into blessing them. I am not alluding to any of those distorted formulations of half-truths that culminate in captivating presentations aimed at manipulative coercion of worshippers. Neither am I standing for those persuasively perfumed promises that lead sincere believers into cycles of disappointment masked as keys to sudden prosperity.

Wake up from your slumber! Pinch yourself if you must! God is not vague, and He certainly can't be arm-twisted into taking shortcuts with you. Yes, even you! Check with millions of churchgoers, and you'll soon realise that distortion of the truth, no matter how garnished it is with sweet talk and gingered-promises, lacks the power to deliver results which are commensurate with the irrefutable promises of God.

Giving, when done right, is a powerful biblical principle that opens doors to receiving. But giving donations alone does not liberate anyone from poverty; receiving alone does not break the back of poverty, even if you do it in church or to your anointed pastor. Take a moment and do the math. Has your godly giving in the last year truly returned as much as could meet all your needs and keep you out of poverty for the next one year? By biblical principles, no one, not even the Levites, should live just receiving, without giving value. You were saved to serve, redeemed to contribute. A life lived merely receiving is a life grossly under-lived. No redeemed soul should solely live on gifts and die, having contributed zero seed, zero succour, and zero value to the world.

Yes, God provides. But He is not a celestial counterfeiter or a rogue ATM. He does not bypass principles to prove His power. What we often call "miracle money" is just the religious repackaging of our craving for magic without effort, blessings without budgeting, increase without diligence. The God who multiplies sown seed still asks, "What do you have in your hand?" Any theology that presents divine wealth without planting seeds, without translating gifts and gifting into value, is not revelation. It is religious entertainment. And if you keep chasing "miracle money," you may end up with empty accounts, high blood pressure, and a borrowed testimony that never shows up in your own life.

Riches don't grow by vibes. They grow by laws, unyielding, unapologetic, and completely unmoved by your hustle, your conviction, or your good intentions. These laws predate your religion. These laws are not housed in stained glass temples or bound by denominational rituals. They're divine protocols etched into the very fabric of creation, not confined to your religious sect or routine. These laws don't flinch at prayer requests. They don't respond to pity parties. They answer only to obedience: measured, meticulous, sometimes maddening obedience. You can't negotiate your way to wealth. It's either you apply the laws or you stay broke. These are not motivational slogans or Sunday sound-bites. They are divine codes wrapped in discipline. They slice through laziness, expose waste, and demand seed, yes, painful seed, before producing any harvest. Growing riches isn't romantic. It's surgical. These laws cut before they multiply. They dissect your habits before they compound your harvest. But once honoured, they activate God's open doors no man can shut and pour flows no drought can dry.

The Non-Negotiable Law of Seed & Bread

There is a law that governs wealth creation, one that's older than banks, budgets, or business schools. The law is not written by the statutes of men, or whispered by the winds of the market. It didn't originate on Wall Street or a financial planner's desk. This is a kingdom principle older than Eden, seeded in Scripture, demonstrated in every harvest since humanity got here at the beginning of time.

This law is blunt, not because it is cruel, but because it is impartial. It doesn't flinch for pity. It doesn't shift for prayer. We're not talking about a law that is gentle. It doesn't bend to emotion or excuse ignorance. The law strips away all financial pretence. It doesn't reward hustle when principle is ignored. It operates whether you believe it or not, and your bank account is already its principal witness.

This law is a mystery that wraps all godly supplies like a two-part currency: one part is bread for your need; the other part is seed for your future. And what you do with each part determines the road you travel, either to scarcity or surplus, either to daily bread only or to enduring future overflows.

The law is brutally straightforward: every income you earn, no matter how small or large, contains two divine components: bread to consume and seed to sow. The bread is for now, it feeds, it clothes, it comforts. But the seed carries tomorrow's wealth; today's answers for future questions. It holds in silence what only sowing can awaken.

This law is brutal but simple because it doesn't negotiate. As old as it is, the law remains unchanged and unbroken: your income contains seed and bread. Touch the seed, starve your own future. Plant the seed, secure a future enwrapped in superabundance. When you treat seed like bread, eat it, spend it, or waste it, you've chosen the road to "just enough" today and "not enough" tomorrow; and automatically incapacitate the future. But if you separate them, consume the bread, separate and plant the seed in a fertile soil, you'll tap into a supernatural pattern of increase that defies economy and circumstance; you'll unlock a divine cycle of multiplication the world can't explain.

Bread is for today. It fuels your journey and provides the necessary comfort. It meets your needs, not necessarily your wants, and certainly not the need that arises because of self-inflicted indulgence. Seed is for tomorrow. It carries potential, promises growth, and triggers divine increase, but only when separated and sown.

This is the principal difference between the road to barely enough and the path to super-abundance. Not luck, not hustle, not even prayer alone can unlock the protocols of lasting riches; but obedience to laws that God set in motion before money had a name.

But herein lays the tragedy: most people eat the whole portion. They spend seed like bread, and consume the future like the present. They eat what should be planted, live off what was meant to grow. And then, in time, they wonder why the increase never comes. They pray for harvests while chewing what could breed it. They fast and shout, tithe and toil, but never separate or sow the one thing that's needful: the seed.

This book isn't about motivational talk or surface-level strategies. It's about realigning your financial life with a spiritual system that never fails. God's financial system is not driven by prayer alone, or positive thinking, or positive confession. It runs on understanding, on honouring the principles of seed and bread.

This book is your map through this law. Not a theory. Not financial fluff. But timeless truth wrapped in Scripture, tested in soil over generations.

It's a spiritual strategy. It's the kingdom code for provision, multiplication, and enduring wealth creation.

Here, you'll see that God's system was never broken; we just never fully lived by it.

So if you've been circling the wilderness of "just enough,"

Or standing at the edge of "not quite,"

It may not be the devil.

It may not be "delay."

If you're tired of financial rollercoasters, stuck in survival mode, or wondering why God isn't "blessing your hustle," the answer may lie in this brutal law of seed and bread that you've been breaking without knowing.

The No-Nonsense Law of Seedtime and Harvest

There are many things in life you can negotiate. You can bargain for time, appeal for mercy, or hustle your way into opportunity. But there's one system that does not flinch, fold, or fail: Seedtime and Harvest.

This is a block of God's Laws that doesn't ask for your permission. It doesn't require your agreement. It simply exists, and operates, whether you believe in it or not.

It is a cluster of God's laws: not a suggestion, not a seasonal sermon. It doesn't care how desperate you are or how long you've waited. It only responds to what you sow. It's not emotional. It doesn't show favouritism. It doesn't care about your intentions, your prayers, or how badly you want it, it only honours what you sow.

It is a law: as sure as gravity, as consistent as sunrise.

Seedtime and harvest are the built-in operating system of the earth. It's how God designed increase, multiplication, and wealth; not by magic, not by prayer, but by motion: the motion of seeds sown in faith, in wisdom, in expectation.

Seedtime is not punishment. It's preparation. It's the part of the journey where patience is tested and trust is required. The law was never meant to cater to emotion. It runs on rhythm, on cycles, on faith in action.

Harvest time will come. That's guaranteed. Though it often feels slow, hidden, and silent, it's not empty. It's working, underground, unseen. The only thing that isn't guaranteed is whether you'll be happy with what shows up as the harvest of what you sowed. Harvest is guaranteed: not a result of luck, not a reward for wishing, but the direct consequence of what you dared to sow.

You may not always know when the harvest will come, but you can be certain it will come, because harvest only responds to a seed.

- No seed, no harvest.
- Wrong seed, wrong harvest.

- Delayed seed, delayed harvest.

You don't harvest what you wish for. You harvest what you sow.

It's that simple. It's that ruthless.

- If you plant nothing, expect nothing.
- If you plant a little, expect a little.
- If you plant wisely, faithfully, and consistently, you tap into a system that always works, even when the process seems slow.

The law works in every area of life. It applies to how you use your time, how you treat people, what you speak, how you build your spiritual life, and where you invest your energy. But nowhere is it more resisted than in finance. We all want God to bless what we spend, but He's only committed to multiplying what we sow. We ask for harvests where we've planted nothing. They tell us to declare "increase" over empty fields. And then we call it a "test of faith" when nothing happens.

But the law didn't break. We just didn't engage it. Seedtime and harvest demand active participation.

It asks:
>What are you planting?
>Where are you planting?
>Are you planting at all?

So the matter isn't whether the system works. The real matter is: what have you been planting?

The Uncompromising Law of Value Exchange (or Giving and Receiving)

"Give, and it shall be given to you…" Yes. But what exactly are you to give? When did it become all and only about money?

If the answer to the law of giving and receiving begins and ends with money handed to a pulpit, a purse, or a personality, then you have misunderstood a divine principle and reduced a powerful spiritual law to a religious transaction. You have been sold counterfeit currency in a kingdom marketplace that demands real value.

What has been done with this Scripture in some quarters where the answer begins and ends with money is a misdiagnosis of liberality, no less criminal than prescribing antibiotics for a broken leg. It doesn't work. It was never designed to. "Give and it shall be given to you" wasn't a veiled pitch for weekly offerings. It was a principle of life, coded into the very ecosystem of creation. Seeds give. Soil gives. Sun gives. Bees give. And in return, fruit comes, flowers bloom, nations are fed.

None of them gave money. But all gave value.

Let me make this clear: Jesus, who taught this lesson, never sold blessing handkerchiefs. He never issued prophetic invoices. He never auctioned healing or traded blessings for envelopes. He gave value: truth, wisdom, healing, presence, time, clarity, vision. And in return, He received what He needed for the journey. When He said, "Give and it shall be given to you," He was not opening a "PayPal link to heaven." He wasn't making a smartly masked presentation for weekly faith-clinic offering. Rather, He was explaining how kingdom ecosystems thrive.

You give kindness, you gain community. You give wisdom, you gain influence. You give skill, you gain income. You give time to growth, you gain relevance. Those are truly "pressed down" and "shaken together" rewards, because what you give is then much less than what you receive in return. That's how heaven's algorithm works.

Value, therefore, is the real substance for kingdom giving; any other thing is either ancillary or made-up. To give value is to give something that solves a problem, meets a need, shifts a system, and fills a gap. And you know the truth? Money is often the reward for that kind of giving, not the material of it. You are not paid because you gave money in church. You are paid because what you gave produced change, and the change produced the pay. That's the kingdom pattern.

You don't pay God to be good to you. When you give in church, you participate in a principle that outlives religion and denomination. However, if you want to grow riches in the godly way, giving is beyond weekly offering. Growing in riches has nothing to do with sowing cash into hypothetical slot machines, and expecting the jackpot of financial miracles; all while ignoring the actual law Jesus laid down: give value, and the value of value will return to you, pressed down, shaken together, running over.

Disastrously, religion mutated that law into a transaction: give X amount to the altar and heaven will wire back 100X in 72 hours. This is not faith. This is a transaction trap! It is spiritualized gambling. And God is not a casino. When giving becomes a formula for divine payout, we miss the point of stewardship and distort the principle of generosity.

Check all around you. Value outperforms currency. Money has limits. Value multiplies. You become a magnet when you give value. Your name enters rooms you haven't stepped into. Your skill outlives seasons. Your work speaks when your mouth is closed. A physician with a powerful skill that heals becomes wealthier than a churchgoer who is taught to give money in order to receive God's blessings, but is never taught to invest in skill or enterprise. This is fundamentally so because the former gives value, the latter gives hope to a system rigged with manipulation. This is the reality of the principle of giving.

Giving is not the problem. Giving as a transaction is. Giving with no value in sight is. When preachers become vending machines, folks become glorified beggars. A church that teaches only about giving money as the way to financial breakthrough, without teaching stewardship, skill development, investment, financial intelligence, and kingdom service, is not growing givers. It is growing beggars in suits. And beggars with Bibles still end up broke, nonetheless. Not because God failed, but because a principle was violated.

If a man gives his last seed every Sunday but never reads a book, never learns a skill, never solves a problem, never mentors anyone, never builds systems, never pursues an enterprise, and never grows his mind, that man is not generous. He is irresponsible.

And God does not reward irresponsibility.

God is a miracle worker. But He is not a miracle dealer. Miracles are interventions, not daily strategies. To live solely by miracle interventions is to announce you have failed in planning. A generation trained to expect breakthroughs without blueprints will forever stay broke. This is the buried truth about the principle of giving.

God gave you hands to work, a mind to create, a spirit to discern, a body to serve. These are your giving instruments. Use them.

Give knowledge to someone struggling. Teach a skill. Build a tool. Write the book. Offer your time. Counsel wisely. Mentor without the camera lights. Pour into ideas that scale. Flow with strategic business development. Give value so potent it becomes unforgettable. That is giving as a principle, as against giving as a transaction.

And when your value fills a room, your rewards will chase you. Employers, clients, nations will chase you with pressed-down rewards; because the principle of giving pays for transformation, not for transaction.

Poverty at its root is not always about lack of money. It is often about the lack of transferable value. When your life has no exportable contribution, your income will reflect your lack of impact. That's the law of giving and receiving. It's harsh. But it's honest. It's tough. But it's unapologetic.

To break poverty, you need to create and distribute value, not just to donate and dance.

Give, but give smart. Sow, but sow sense. You are not meant to bankrupt your family in hopes of magic money. You're meant to partner with God by building value that heaven can multiply.

Stop dropping money at altars, hoping for Ferrari miracles when your business plan is still in your dreams. God is not mocked. You don't grow financially through donation alone. You grow by creating transformational value. You grow by adding value to your domain.

Give time. Give wisdom. Give excellence. Give service. Give creation. And watch the heavens respond.

Because value is the one offering heaven reimburses in full plus bonus, and without repentance.

This is the unapologetic law of giving and receiving. And the compensation for giving in value ensures that givers never have to question the authenticity of the law whenever their results show up.

How the Laws Relate and Operate

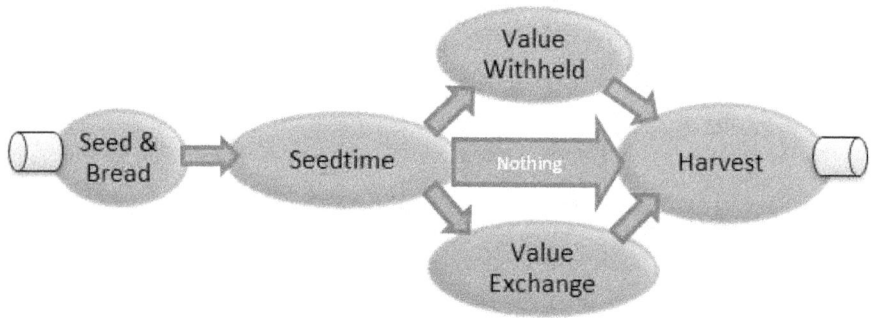

How the laws relate

The law of Seed & Bread is where the journey begins. God gives seed to the sower and bread for food, but the wise know not to confuse the two. Bread is for today's sustenance; seed is for tomorrow's abundance. The moment we consume the seed meant to be planted, we mortgage our future for the comfort of now. It is from this sacred separation that all legal and godly wealth-building flows, whether it begins from you or from someone else. Your seed is the raw potential that must be intentionally sown, not flaunted. Without honouring this law, you may work hard, earn much, and still find your hands mysteriously empty.

Then comes Seedtime, the law that mocks laziness and rewards diligence. The seed you preserved must enter the soil of value creation: a business, an investment, a relationship of mutual value benefit. Here, time and patience do their work, for no harvest comes overnight.

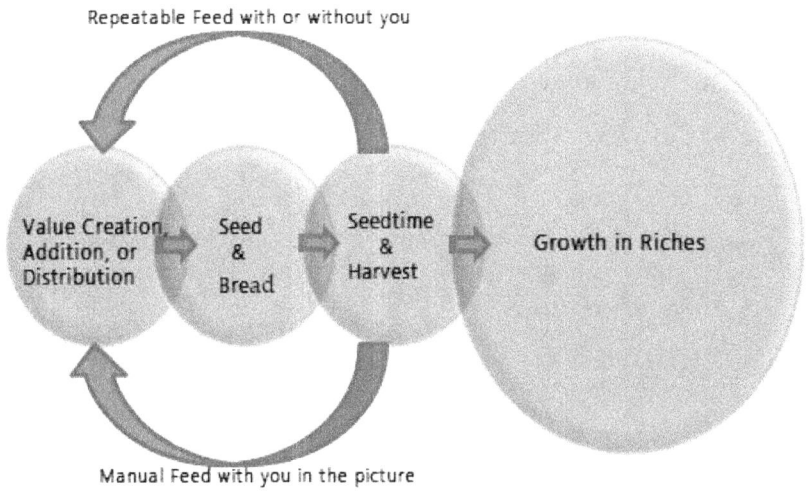

How the laws operate

And when the sowing is done at the right time and in the right soil, the law of Value Exchange steps in: when what you have meets the needs of others in a fair and profitable exchange. This is where harvest happens. This is where seed sown is multiplied. This is where riches grow roots, not from hoarding, but from flowing. Seed leads to sowing; sowing becomes the catalyst for value exchange; value exchange leads to reaping; and reaping becomes the fuel for greater value exchange. Break one link in this chain, and riches remain a dream. Honour them all, and wealth becomes a system, not an event. The more value you can set in motion, able to flow repeatedly with or without your shadow in the room, the greater the riches that will find their way to you.

Chapter 2

The Non-Negotiable Law of Seed and Bread

Let's take a moment to dig. Let's journey beneath the surface of a Scripture many quote but few truly mine. Hidden in its folds are divine gems, not loud, not flashy, but potent. These are treasures wrapped in ancient protocols, waiting for discerning eyes and hungry hearts. So come with me… let's unearth what others have skimmed over. What they read, we'll reveal. What they recite, we'll extract. This isn't just Bible study, it's spiritual excavation:

> **Now he that ministereth seed to the sower both minister bread for your food, and multiply your seed sown, and increase the fruits of your righteousness.** 2 Cor 9:10 (KJV)

Take a thoughtful look at the verse again, this time, somewhat slowly:

> **Now he that ministereth seed to the sower both minister bread for your food, and multiply your seed sown, and increase the fruits of your righteousness.**

The above verse unveils the dominant principles of provision that you need to learn, embrace, and fulfil if you must access the packages of abundance that are available to kingdom citizens on life's voyage.

Read the verse again, this time with rapt attention. Observe that there are three layers at which God administers supplies, with one layer separated from the next by the heavily pregnant word **'and'**.

> **Now he that ministereth seed to the sower both minister bread for your food, and multiply your seed sown, and increase the fruits of your righteousness.**

God does three things here:

- ministers seed to the sower and bread for your food,
- and multiply your seed sown,
- and increase the fruits of your righteousness

Layer 1: Layer of Basic Supply

> *Now he that ministereth seed to the sower both minister bread for your food,*

This is the most rudimentary level of God's provision to anyone. Here, God ministers two different things: seed and bread. The word 'both' is an old way of saying 'also' or 'simultaneously.' The verse begins by saying, **'He that ministers seed to the sower also ministers bread for your food'**.

What are the implications of this first and basic layer of supply?

The first implication is that God, who ministers seed, also ministers bread to you at this layer of basic supply. This is because your supplies get released in expectation that you would be a sower and an eater. A docile mind embraces the '**bread for your food**' part of that holy writ but snubs the '**seed to the sower**' part. But, as a sower of seed gets administered some portions of bread, which he is to eat, the eater of bread is also apportioned some measures of seed, which he is supposed to sow.

Now, God's ministration to you at this layer comes with two distinct entities: **seed** and **bread**. These two entities are not necessarily **separate** from the source or **separated** at the point of ministration.

This is the first and most crucial matter here, and the foundation upon which true abundance is built, line upon line, layer upon layer. God regularly supplies you with seed and bread, expecting you to recognise each for what it is and dispense each according to its unique mission.

There are different parcels of ministrations that God employs to dispense supplies to citizens of His kingdom, and each comes for unique purposes and with specific terms and conditions. But when God ministers provision at this layer of supply, it comes as a block of seed and bread. His ministration is not limited to bread only, neither is it restricted to seed only. The two are lumped together when God ministers provision at the layer of basic supply. It doesn't matter whether you receive your provision as a salary or benefit or bonus or profit or royalty–it contains seed and bread. The seed quota is meant for sowing, while the bread portion is meant for food. The seed quota does not refer to tithe or offering or charitable donations. The seed quota is something you need to sow into your own field, without which Layer 2 of God's provision becomes redundant, weakened, and worthless.

Unfortunately, throngs of folks consume all the provisions that come to them at this layer every week, every month; including many Christians who faithfully disburse a part of their earnings as tithes and make regular offerings and donations. A large percentage of folks eat their seeds with their bread. Many do not even recognise that their provision comes from God and that it contains seed and bread: seed for sowing, bread for sustenance. By eating all the supplies that come to you at this layer of basic supply, you leave nothing to carry forward to the second layer of God's provision. Yet, the second layer of God's provision is designed and programmed to receive its own supplies solely from the seed garnered at the first layer.

When you consume all your income at the layer of basic supply (even if you earn 7 figures per annum), you automatically choose the lane to hardly enough on the road to future poverty. Treading this path inevitably restricts your supplies to the basic level only, at the first layer of God's provision. Your basic supplies through salary, earnings, first layer profit, allowance and such likes may continue or even increase a little in due course, but they will dry up when you are out of a job, unable to work or retire. While God intends to make provisions available at 3 layers, consuming all your income automatically restricts His provisions to the layer of basic supply and cuts off deliveries at the remaining 2 layers. By consuming everything in the package of your earning, you unescapably seal your fate to the lane of impending lack, alleviated poverty, and warehoused scarcity, and that without remedy.

While God faithfully supplies seed and bread at this first layer, it is your responsibility to administer them according to the principles that govern prosperity before you can expect amplified provisions, which He faithfully keeps beyond this layer of basic supplies.

Layer 2: Layer of Multiplication

…, and multiply your seed sown,

In this advanced layer of provision, God multiplies seeds. This second layer is not meant for basic supplies at all. Rather, it is designed for the multiplication of those precious seeds administered to you at the first layer.

God does not send fresh seeds at this layer? Rather, He multiplies the seed that you separate from the provision that comes to you in layer 1 (layer of basic supply), and later sow. By principle, God releases layer 1 supply as a lumped quantity. By principle, the receiver also has the responsibility to separate those precious seeds from their bread associates, and sow the separated seeds. God does not separate the seed from the bread before dispensing it, because that is your responsibility.

He does not keep separated seed in safe custody because that is your responsibility. God does not sow the seed on your behalf because that is your responsibility. But God sends the initial provision at the layer of basic supply and then leaves you with the responsibility of conforming to necessary principles so that He can multiply the seed you sow from layer one.

The seed to sow comes from the provision (or ministration) that God sends to you in the layer of basic supply, and this does not refer to your tithe or offering at all. Tithe and offering have their roles, but they differ completely from the seed that God commits Himself to multiplying in layer 2 of this crucial principle. When you faithfully steward your tithe and offering, you unlock the principle that opens the windows of heaven and the principle that fertilizes your soil. However, when heaven sends rain on your fertilised soil, there is nothing to multiply if the soil lacks sown seed. There is nothing to bud. There is nothing to blossom. There is nothing to reproduce after its kind, even though your soil is fertile and doesn't lack rainfall.

As a matter of fact, rain does not discriminate. Fertiliser does not show favouritism. But weed readily propagates itself on your fertile and well-watered but empty field; when you sow no seeds on it. Therefore, tithe and offering are not sufficient for financial prosperity. You need to have a field (or fields) in which your separated seed (from Layer one) gets sown so that God can also find what to multiply in Layer two.

Separated and sown seed is so crucial to your financial advancement that without it, you go against unbendable principles of prosperity, restrict God's supplies to Layer 1 only, blockade God's promised provision in layer 2, and confine yourself to the lane that produces insufficiency in its trail and future poverty as its outcome.

Layer 3: Layer of Increase

..., and increase the fruits of your righteousness

This is the most tremendous, most superior layer of God's provision, where He increases your supplies in the most amazing way! At this layer of God's provision, financial stewardship and accountability becomes a blended beam of righteousness for anyone who is compliant to this point. And here, your righteousness gets bountifully rewarded. Unfortunately, there are only a few folks who make it to this point, despite God's unwavering commitment to these principles.

As seeds become multiplied in layer 2, many recipients typically increase their consumption also, therefore confining themselves to provisions at the layer of basic supply and layer of multiplication. But the principles of prosperity at the layer of multiplication, according to Scriptures, confer on your shoulders much more discipline and far greater responsibilities rather than more consumption and extra liabilities.

When your seed gets multiplied in layer 2, the size of your bread also becomes increased. But it takes discipline to realize that multiplied seed is not equal to multiplied consumption.

When your seed multiplies, your bread has the propensity to multiply. But you must eat cautiously when multiplication manifests, *"as if a knife were at your throat,"* so that consumption only gets your consent for addition but not the luxury of multiplication. Multiplied seed furnishes multiplied bread to eat, but you must keep your consumption within the boundaries of addition, not over-indulged to spiral upward into the edges of multiplication. Let multiplied bread unfold the opportunity of storage, and open you up to more open-handedness, but it must not be allowed to stir up multiplied consumption.

Multiplied seed must lead you to increased sowing. Increased sowing demands more fields, more purposeful expansion into new and additional fields for much more sowing; and even further extension into new territories. From here, there awaits extraordinary increment through exponential powers and compound interest, far beyond mere multiplication that is available in Layer 2.

What layer are you at? What is keeping there? What layer are you aiming for? God's commitment is resolute to anyone who will follow His principles. It's left to you to decide where to voyage: whether on the highway to future lack and warehoused poverty or on the byway to abundance and a legacy of lasting riches.

Chapter 3

The No-Nonsense Law of Seedtime and Harvest

Now, kindly read that opening verse again. But this time, don't just skim the surface. Peer through the lines and listen for the silent rhythm of seasons buried within the multi-layered laws of God's provision. There's more here than meets the eye, timelines, patterns, divine rhythms tucked between the commas.

> **"Now he that ministereth seed to the sower both minister bread for your food, and multiply your seed sown, and increase the fruits of your righteousness."**

First, God does not activate all provisions for layer 1, layer 2, and layer 3 in the same season. There is a season for the ministration of first layer's seed and bread, after which there is a pause for the sower to sow his/her seed.

The sower sometimes takes a while to separate or save sufficient seeds (in quantity or quality), and possibly some additional time to prepare the field. Afterward, he proceeds to sow separated seeds at a favourable seedtime (or sowing season). Then the sower waits in hope and faith. In fulfilling His own side of the principle, God subsequently multiplies sown seed in the interval between seedtime (season) and harvest (season). This subsequently ushers the sower into the season of harvest, which ends the complete Season 1.

This cycle continues for a sower who wishes to access provisions beyond layer 2.

The interval between a sower's seedtime and his harvest depends largely on the seedtype: quarterly, biannual, annual, biennial, or perennial. This crucial matter of the season of your invested seed will be expanded later in this book. For now, the simple way to simplify a season is that some investments mature in three months, some take three years, and some require thirty seasons to fully compound into a **financial fortress**.

So, from this golden verse, a sower can touch three flavours of God's provision, and three seasons of personal responsibilities in the intervals.

- ❖ God's flavour of provision
    - ➢ Flavour of ministration
    - ➢ Flavour of multiplication
    - ➢ Flavour of exponential increase

In between God's flavours, we have the sower's seasons of responsibilities, determined by factors like readiness, time before seed separation, interval of field preparation, and actual sowing. So, a sower must work with intention to activate the next flavour of God's provision in the next phase.

- ❖ Man's seasons of (or intervals for) responsibilities
  - ➤ Seedtime1 (Interval between ministration and multiplication)
  - ➤ Seedtime2 (Interval between multiplication and exponential increase)
  - ➤ Seedtime3 (Interval between exponential increase and financial fortress)

Here is a single description for each of the seasons and intervals involved:

Season 1 (Season of Ministration):

Procedures:

i. God ministers seed and bread (and pauses)
ii. Individual receives administered provision
iii. **Seedtime 1** (Interval 1 for administered seed): The sower separates ministered seed from bread, eats only the bread (consumes, stores, shares, or donates), prepares his field, and sows the separated seed in anticipation of God's multiplying power.

Season 2 (Season of Multiplication):

Procedures:

i. God multiplies sown seed (and pauses again).

ii. **Harvest 2** (Interval 2a for the harvest of multiplied provision): The sower receives more instalments of Layer 1 provision and also harvests multiplied provisions from layer 2).

iii. **Seedtime 2** (Seedtime for multiplied seed): The sower separates multiplied seed from multiplied bread, eats only the bread (consumes, stores, shares, or donates), prepares his field, and sows the multiplied seed.

Season 3 (Season of Exponential Increase):

Procedures::

i. God exponentially increases re-sown, multiplied seed (and pauses again)

ii. **Harvest 3** (Interval 3a for the harvest of exponential increase): The sower receives more instalments of Layer 1 provision, harvests multiplied provision from Layer 2, and also harvests exponential increase from Layer 3).

iii. **Seedtime 3** (Seedtime for exponentially increased seed): The sower separates exponentially increased seed from bread, eats only the compounded bread (consume, store, share, donate), and turns the compounded seed into a fortress (re-sows, expands, acquires, mentors, sponsors, funds startups, donates, hands over to the next generation).

This is the law of seedtime and harvest, which never ceases. It doesn't respect your race. It doesn't disrespect your religion. It just responds to whatever you sow. Those who understand this law can turn in their separated seeds for another sowing every 3 to 6 months, but some people who disregard the law have separated no seed for sowing in the last 30 months.

Your interval of responsibility is directly proportional to the length of your obedience in harvest and seedtime. So, your financial growth doesn't just depend on the quantity or quality of seed sown, it also has a lot to do with your interval of responsibility and God's incremental power at that layer of your obedience.

If the above explanation is too wordy, you may be quick to grasp the mathematical equation below:

$$Gkr = \frac{Ti * Sq * Gp}{St}$$

$$Ti = Th + Tse + Tpf + Tso$$

Where:

Gkr = Growth in Kingdom Riches
Ti = Time interval (how long it takes to comply with the law of seedtime)
Th = Time to Harvest previous provision

Tse = Time to Separate ministered seed

Tpf = Time to Prepare investment Field

Tso = Time to Sow separated seed

Sq = Seed quality and quantity

Gp = God's incremental Power (at the level of your obedience)

St = Seed type (maturity time in years - annual, biennial, perennial)

To highlight the points again:

Growth in Kingdom Riches is a function of four principal factors:

- The time it takes to obey financial principles of seedtime, which includes the responsibilities of separating administered seed, preparing the right investment field, and sowing the separated seed.
- The quality and quantity of seed sown,
- God's incremental power at the layer of a sower's obedience (there is addition @Layer1, multiplication @Layer2, and exponential @Layer3)
- Seed type (investment maturity time in years - annual, biennial, perennial)

If mathematical equations are not your thing, there are a few diagrams that further illustrate the principles upon which the different layers and individual responsibilities stand in subsequent chapters.

For a perpetual Eater of Seed, growth is stunted, because seed, the crucial parameter coming from him, is zero. So, a perpetual consumer of seed is gradually sliding into poverty (knowingly or unknowingly) regardless of how much he earns today or how potent God's incremental power is.

Compounding adds new gains to the existing base, thereby, increasing seed quantity and sometimes quality. This is the reason there is no better way to grow riches than compounding, as far as a sower's responsibilities are concerned.

The Dimensions of the Law of Seedtime and Harvest

Below is a list of some dimensions to the time-tested, time honoured law of seedtime and harvest that we can glean from the Bible. Besides being a dimension of the law of harvest, each of these stands as a principle on its own.

    i.   **Seasons of sowing and reaping will continue as long as the earth remains.**
- Implications:
    a. The law never takes a day off; even when you take 10 years off.

b. While you're hesitating or eating your seeds, others are planting and activating kingdom riches.

   c. Those who fail to plant will supplicate when sowers dominate.

ii. **You reap today what was once sown (by you or someone else).**
   - <u>Implications</u>:
      a. You're harvesting today those seeds you planted or denied years ago.
      b. Your current results/bank account is a report card of past decisions you or someone ahead of you made before now.
      c. Whatever you reap today was once planted (ignorantly or by choice).

iii. **You reap the same in kind as you sow.**
   - <u>Implications</u>:
      a. Stop expecting peaches when you're planting peanuts.
      b. The short-sighted Fool's math: 1 seed = 1 seed.
      c. The Farsighted Wise's math: 1 seed = a forest.

iv. **You reap in a different season than you sow.**
   - <u>Implications</u>:

a. Harvest doesn't show up immediately, it arrives in its own season.
b. Weak people quit after 3 months. The greats keep planting through 30 storms.
c. Good or bad, your children are on the waiting line.

v. **You reap in proportion to what you sow**.
  - Implication:
    a. Your harvest matches your planting in proper ratio.
    b. Plant little, reap little. Plant much, reap much.
    c. Small seed + obedience is better than zero seed + intention.

vi. **You reap more than you sow**.
  - Implication:
    a. Your "not enough" contains God's raw material for overflow.
    b. Your small seed + God's miracle = A harvest you can't contain.
    c. That "quick fix" may cost you 100x returns.

vii. **You reap the full harvest of the good only if you persevere, but weeds naturally come to fruition on their own.**

- Implication:
    a. Good crops demand work, but weeds grow automatically.
    b. Planting good seed isn't enough; hard work must follow.
    c. Spectators involuntarily grow weeds, investors deliberately grow wheat.

viii. **You reap the harvest of self-propagated weeds if you fail to sow good seed.**
- Implication:
    a. No planting? Congratulations, you just farmed failure.
    b. Weed's comeback begins the instant you stop planting seed.
    c. "The bad" and "the ugly" will like to lurk around the future of your voyage: the only antidote is to sow "the good" today.

ix. **You cannot do anything to change the last harvest, but you can do something about the next.**
- Implication:
    a. Last year's failure expired at midnight.
    b. You can't fix last season's crop failure, but all hope is not lost.

            c. You can dominate next season with today's seeds.

   x. **Today holds the harvest of yesterday, as well as the seed of tomorrow**.
        ○ Implication:
            a. Right now is your harvest from yesterday's planting.
            b. Make today your seed moment for tomorrow's abundance.
            c. You didn't ordain past seed, but you must dictate future harvest.

This law isn't fair, it's faithful. It has nothing to do with fairness. It will not apologize for your famine if you ignore it. And it will not deny your increase if you honour it. It is a no-nonsense, no-fluff, and non-negotiable law. You can fight it, disregard it, or flow with it; it's your choice. But you cannot escape it. You may ignore or engage it. But you cannot get away from its outcome. As long as the earth remains, seedtime and harvest shall not cease.

This is not superstition. It's not hype. This is not a feel-good message to encourage sowing. It's a spiritual law, grounded in Genesis, repeated throughout Scripture, and visible in every part of life: You reap what you sow, later than you sow, and more than you sow.

The law is emphatic. It doesn't reward good intentions. It doesn't respond to noise. It responds to seed: strategic, intentional, obedient seed.

So whether you're managing your money, building a business, raising a family, or growing your faith, the principle remains the same: respect seedtime and be rewarded at the harvest. So, you either make it your ever-potent weapon for wealth creation or reduce it to your fragile excuse for poverty.

Chapter 4

The Uncompromising Law of Value Exchange

Return to that verse, not as a reader, but as a seeker. Read it like you're holding something holy in your hands, like a son returning to the inheritance he almost missed.

> "Now he that ministereth seed to the sower both minister bread for your food, and multiply your seed sown, and increase the fruits of your righteousness."

Take note again that God **multiplies seed sown** during the intervals between layers 1 and 2; and **increases seed re-sown** (seed-base plus seed-gain) during the intervals between layers 2 and 3.

Now, the verse has brought us to another vantage point where we must distinguish seed from seed. The first seed is **separated seed** (separated from bread), while the second is **seed sown** (or sown seed). The two are not the same. Separated seed does not command God's multiplication or exponential power, sown seed does. If all you accomplish is separated seed, your effort is just as good as an *attempted-prosperity*. You have only made an attempt at growing riches. You may separate mountains of seeds in savings, but the best you can attract is fractional additions by your financial institution. But your separated seed is always at the risk of remaining in savings until it's spent, or spoilt, or lost.

While **separated seed** is the first stair of obedience, **seed sown** (or sown seed) is the real activator of God's multiplying and compounding powers. I hope you can see the difference clearly.

There is one question that I need to answer here, on the substance of sown seed.

What exactly is your seed sown; capable of multiplication and exponential increase?

First cue is, separated seed does not look like seed sown. Both are called seeds, but they wear different garments and trigger different effects. Separated seed wears the garments of **savings**: funds, reserves, capital, harvest, and, in every way, looks very much like bread, which could be easily consumed. Sown seed, on the other hand, wears the garment of **value**: products and services, business ventures, investments, shares, holdings, equities, properties etc., which could only be converted into currency before being spent.

Whether you're rich or poor, Asian or Latino, highly anointed or newly converted, value exchange is the shared language that growing true kingdom riches truly understands. When separated seed becomes a regular occurrence in the management of your income, value exchange must also become the common denominator of your multiplication and exponential increase. Otherwise, you may spend your separated seed in times of need, keep it almost stagnant in the bank, erode it in the motions of inflation, or entrust it into the care of swindlers. So, it is essential to turn separated seed into seed sown in a proven system of value exchange.

Look at the law we misunderstand and violate repeatedly:

> "Give, and it will be given to you: good measure, pressed down, shaken together, and running over will be put into your bosom. For with the same measure that you use, it will be measured back to you." Luke 6:38 (NKJV)

Lazy/Misinformed/Disinformed Interpretation and activation Strategy:

- Give offering/donation => Receive surprise money => Do thanksgiving
- Give more offering/donation => Receive surprise job/deal for money => Do thanksgiving
- Give painful offering/donation => Receive financial breakthrough => Do thanksgiving

Kingdom Interpretation and activation Strategy:

- Give value => Receive money equivalent => Steward your return

- Give more value => Receive money equivalent => Steward your return
- Spread more value more => Receive money equivalent => Steward your return

Kingdom riches don't respond to religious gymnastics; they respond to kingdom laws, and value exchange is one of those foremost laws. So, to the question: "What exactly should be your **seed sown** that's capable of multiplication and exponential increase?" I attempted to address this question in the first chapter, that "Give, and it shall be given to you…" is more of a call to a system of value exchange than of weekly offering.

Too many people have been taught that giving is measured only in cash and envelopes. But the kingdom of God does not run on currency, it runs on current. It thrives on the transfer of value. Exchange of value is a divine energy that flows when essence is exchanged for essence. When we confine the law of giving and receiving to the narrow lane of passing coins and dollar bills from one hand to another, we mistake the river for the bucket. We reduce a life-giving principle into a mere transaction, and then wonder why it feels empty. The law of value exchange is an invitation to participate in kingdom ecosystem where your giving gives life to your gathering. And no! It is not to give offering so that you can receive your promotion.

Look at the unspoken procedure of creation: The sun does not send an invoice for its light. The soil does not demand payment before it nurtures the seed. The bee, in its silent, purposeful work, does not pollinate for a fee. They simply give their irreducible essence, their light, their life, their labour, and in that profound surrender, the entire world is fed, clothed, and sustained. In return, the givers receive superior essence of life to give more. This is the original economy. Creation thrives because everything is created to contribute value and receive the lifeblood that produces more value (in good measure). This is the law written into the fabric of all things: life begets life through the conduit of value exchange.

Now, behold the Master Economist, Jesus. He never sold access. He never packaged grace into tiers. He never presented a miracle menu with pricing on the side. His economy was one of profound value exchange: truth for freedom, healing for faith, presence for belonging. He gave His very substance, and in return, received the substance needed for His journey. When He said, "Give, and it will be given to you," He was not launching a heavenly fundraising strategy. He was pulling back the curtain on the universe's operational system.

He was saying: Your value is your greatest asset. Offer it, your skill, your time, your compassion, your wisdom, into the ecosystem of need around you. Watch how heaven's machinery engages to honour that exchange. The soil will honour the seed. The harvest will honour the sower. But you must first understand: you are not funding His mission. You are deploying your essence in His kingdom. And that changes everything.

Giving donations (to the poor, to charity, to your church) when you also have value to exchange will produce results in any location and currency. Giving donations with no value to exchange will disappoint you now and for life, regardless of who is cheering you on with "it's gonna be well with you".

I will highlight the broad areas of the system of value exchange in this section and discuss its vital connection to Christian giving in another chapter. But for now at this foundational level, let me reiterate that anyone who takes the striking instruction to "sow" or to "Give, and it shall be given to you…" as a call limited to weekly offerings and monthly donations is narrow in execution and more likely constricted in results.

Below are clear and relatable categories of Value Exchange, all explained in a way that any layperson can connect with.

A. Turn Your Separated Seed Into Value Creation

Value creation is about birthing something that didn't exist before, a product, service, idea, or experience that solves a problem or meets a need. You're starting from scratch; bringing a solution, service, or product into existence where there was none. While there are hundreds of examples employing various skills and talents to create value, these 10 highlight mere glimpses, and should equip you with even more inspiration to locate those separated seeds and your own abilities in wealth creation through the lens of kingdom value exchange (or seed sown).

i. Developing a mobile app for exam success tailored to your country's curriculum.
ii. Writing a children's book that teaches values and sells at schools or online.
iii. Opening a mini car wash near a popular street where there's no existing service.
iv. Launching a YouTube channel that teaches practical skills like sewing, baking, or budgeting.
v. Creating a custom skincare product for people with sensitive skin.
vi. Hosting paid webinars or online classes on how to start a side hustle.
vii. Creating a daily devotional podcast for youth on Spotify.
viii. Launching a pet-sitting business in neighbourhoods with lots of pet owners.
ix. Inventing a reusable food wrap made from organic materials.
x. Designing custom T-shirts with quotes that resonate with a niche audience.

Value creation is the birthing room of wealth. You step into riches by stepping up to solve unmet needs. Every innovation, every godly idea acted upon, is a sown seed that can grow into generational wealth.

B. Turn Your Separated Seed Into Value Addition

Value addition means improving something that already exists: making it better, faster, safer, cheaper, or more beautiful. Value addition is how you stand out in a noisy marketplace. It turns average products into irresistible offers. God gives seed, but what you do with the seed determines whether you eat today or harvest for life. Of the countless ways people add value to existing products, services, platforms and systems, these ten examples are simply windows, brief but brilliant, into what's possible, and they're shared to ignite within you a deeper recognition of your own capacity to turn your separated seed into building blocks of wealth through kingdom-minded value addition.

i. Redesigning a website to make it more user-friendly and attractive.
ii. Adding whipped cream and caramel drizzle to plain coffee to make a premium version.
iii. Packaging local farm produce neatly in baskets/cartons for export or easy sale at supermarkets.
iv. Polishing resumes, rewriting dull CVs, and optimizing LinkedIn profiles for job seekers.
v. Converting eBooks into audiobooks for busy professionals.
vi. Adding nutritious and diet ingredients to a popular food item.
vii. Adding online payment features to a local vendor's business.
viii. Repackaging local spices in hygienic, resalable, exportable containers.

ix. Editing old sermons or talks into short, engaging reels for social media; or turning raw videos into edited, high-quality content for social media influencers.

x. Turning a handmade item into a customized, limited-edition product.

C. Turn Your Separated Seed Into Value Distribution

Value distribution involves taking a product, service, or idea and ensuring it reaches more people. What you're doing is helping others to access what already exists by delivering, marketing, repackaging, recommending, or spreading.

There are hundreds of ways people turn value distribution into wealth. These ten are just a sneak peek, enough to spark something inside you, to help you recognize that your own abilities to spread and supply either yours or other people's products and services, too, are keys to unlocking kingdom prosperity when exchanged with purpose.

i. Becoming an affiliate marketer and promoting others' products online.

ii. Becoming a delivery rider to get food from restaurants to homes.

iii. Sharing educational content on social media that brings awareness to useful tools.

iv. Distributing clean water in sachets to event venues and construction sites.

v. Creating YouTube summaries of business books, making them accessible to non-readers.

vi. Partnering with local artisans to list their services on Google Maps and business directories; or sell their crafts internationally via Etsy or Shopify.

vii. Becoming a dropshipper for home goods, clothing, or accessories.

viii. Creating TikTok videos explaining complex products in simple terms.

ix. Distributing health and wellness products to working-class professionals.

x. Creating an online job board where employers and job seekers meet.

You don't have to be the creator. Even the best product will rot in silence if it doesn't reach the right hands. Value stuck in one place remains buried treasure. It is distribution that unlocks its real worth. All you need to start is the will to distribute what others have created. Once you start, value distribution becomes the highway of wealth.

D. Turn Your Separated Seed Into Value Partnership

Value Partnership is a strategic collaboration between two or more people, organizations, or entities that bring different strengths to the table and combine them to achieve a shared goal, especially in ways that produce impact, income, or influence that neither could achieve alone.

It's not just about working together; it's about working wisely, intentionally, and divinely aligned. One person brings the seed, and another tills the soil. One writes the vision; another runs with it. One has the voice; the other builds the platform. Together, they both reap a harvest that would have been impossible in isolation.

Let me add that these ten examples barely scratch the surface of the ocean of potential flowing through partnership. Yet they shine like torches, lighting the path for you to discover your own gifts, and wield them as instruments of wealth in the divine economy of kingdom value exchange.

i. Business with a friend who has capital while you have skills – one funds it, the other runs it.
ii. Joint YouTube channel or podcast – you're good at speaking, they handle editing and posting.
iii. Co-authoring a Book – You bring the content; someone else brings publishing experience.
iv. Teaming up as a writer and a tech-savvy friend. The writer brings ideas and content; the tech friend turns it into a blog,

eBook, or email sequence. Together, they monetize what would've stayed in a journal.

v. A stay-at-home parent partners with a busy entrepreneur. The parent handles customer service or admin tasks remotely, while the entrepreneur runs the field operations. One manages the back-end, the other, the front-end.

vi. A kingdom-minded designer partners with a Christian influencer. The tailor sews modest, stylish outfits; the influencer wears and shares it on social media.

vii. A farmer collaborates with a logistics partner. One grows the produce; the other distributes it to retailers or end-consumers. Together, they eliminate waste and maximize sales.

viii. Two Friends Start a Drop-Shipping Business. One is detail-oriented and handles sourcing and logistics; the other is people-oriented and handles marketing and customer interaction.

ix. The landowner provides space, the builder develops rental apartments or farming initiatives, and they share profits or ownership.

x. An anointed speaker partners with a book publisher. The speaker provides transformational content; the publisher handles editing, printing, and global distribution; so, kingdom impact is multiplied.

In kingdom economy, value partnership is scriptural. Moses needed Aaron. Paul had Timothy. Peter beckoned to partners; otherwise he could have lost a large portion of his boat-sinking catch. No lone ranger thrives in full capacity of kingdom purpose or prosperity. The oil flows where alignment meets assignment.

With DIY mindsets and self-made man myths flooding the world, value partnership is the forgotten weapon of exponential fruitfulness. It says: You don't have to do everything. Just bring your value to the table, and partner wisely with those who can amplify it.

It is okay to give donations, Christian stewardship demands it. But look and see beyond the imbalance orientation that **"seed sown"** and **"Give, and it shall be given to you…"** are all about weekly offering as you've been told possibly since childhood. You don't need to be everywhere, but you must plug in somewhere. Whether you sow into creating, enhancing, partnering on, or transferring value, God blesses working systems of value, and money is always looking for the hand that delivers the most real, consistent, and helpful value to others.

Money is never missing; it's merely hidden: buried in plain sight, camouflaged in people, wrapped in problems, veiled in skills, locked up in ideas, tucked inside systems, and submerged in products and services. It doesn't fall from the sky or rain from heaven like manna. Instead, money answers to those who dare to create, add, or distribute value. If you're praying for provision but ignoring value exchange, you're playing religious games with your destiny. Wealth does not obey wishful-thinking or positive confession; it obeys the ancient, unfailing laws of value exchange kept in such sacred writs like:

> **"give, and it shall be given to you…"** and

> **"…and multiply your seed sown, and increase the fruits of your righteousness."**

The tragedy is, many believers seek the anointing but not the understanding. They cry for miracles while sitting on goldmines of unrefined opportunities. They dance around altars but ignore their own altar of diligence. When God speaks on their personal prayer altar, He speaks in principles. But many prefer what the pastor says to what the principles of God's provision say; because we yearn for magic without work and desire increase without industry.

Chapter 5

The Mirage of "Miracle Money"

Miracle money, as it's often preached today, is a sugar-coated sedative for indolence, a spiritualised disguise for financial irresponsibility, and an insult to the laws God Himself set in motion. It flatters poverty but never frees it. It pacifies hunger but never feeds it. It dangles the illusion of harvest where no seed was sown and calls it divine favour. That's not faith. That's fantasy.

The toxic theology of "prophetic money" has succeeded in funding the poverty and misery of many church folks so intolerably, except that the only exceptions are the "anointed" cons, together with their cronies. It promises divine dollars but delivers deep debt. Rise from that stupor or get ready to stomach acute frustration. If you must grow riches the godly way, you've got to break free from that financial sleepwalking and wake up to your money reality.

You may shout hallelujah for hours. You can run laps around the altar until your sweat becomes incense. You may fall down from a preacher's touch so hard the ushers need stretchers to carry you. But if you ignore the principle of sowing and reaping or the principle of seed and bread, you will remain broke, emotionally elated, but spiritually exhausted and financially stranded.

God is not a magician. The heavens are not an ATM. And prayer is not a replacement for planting.

There's a silent contradiction happening in modern-day Christianity globally. We gather in numbers, asking and waiting for God to multiply what we refuse to sow. We plead the blood, yet ignore the budget. We quote "My God shall supply all my needs," while violating the very laws that unlock His full-blown supplies.

The Bible hasn't changed:

> "He who sows sparingly shall reap sparingly…" 2 Cor 9:6 (NKJV)

> "As long as the earth remains, seedtime and harvest shall not cease." Gen 8:22 (NKJV)

> "Give, and it will be given to you: good measure, pressed down, shaken together, and running over will be put into your bosom. For with the same measure that you use, it will be measured back to you." Luke 6:38 (NKJV)

It's not a mystery. It's a model. You don't need an impartation to access financial prosperity; you need an instruction. You don't need a mantle;

you need a mindset. You don't need a "man of God" to spit on your forehead; you need understanding and follow-through with biblically accurate financial principles.

There's a tragedy. Where very few who are serious about accessing financial prosperity are learning investment strategies, multitudes whose quests for riches turn out to be "mere wishes" are learning new anointing slogans. Where those few prioritize attending financial literacy seminars, multitudes attend "Open Heaven Breakthrough Fire Explosion Nights."

The informed save and invest; the flippant shout and dance. The sincere ones study biblical economics, while the shallow ones queue up for another "prophetic seed." The resolute few invest in skill acquisition and business strategy, but the superficial lot tithe into holy water and prayer shawls. And then we wonder why the financial gap between them and the others keeps widening.

We blame demons. They build discipline. We compound church activities. They compound interests. We anoint work tools. They hold vision boards. The results are not mysterious, they're mathematical.

It's not that God isn't faithful. It's that we've become financially foolish. It is that we became reckless in stewardship, giving room for unstable men to twist the word of God and to prey on our foolishness for their personal gain.

Heaven responds to principles, not pity. God honours patterns, not pressure. Prosperity is not a by-product of volume in prayer. It's a by-product of obedience to the principles of seed and bread, seedtime and harvest, giving and receiving.

The Scripture is clear. The treasure of riches is in your seed. It must not be eaten. It must be sown in your field and at the right season, not given to any "man of God".

But we have turned our churches into echo chambers of entitlement. So, we expect to reap what we've never planted. We want harvests with no habits. We want provision with no process. We want manna with no management. And when the miracle doesn't come, we blame God, the economy, or village witches.

But the truth is painful: our prayer noise has become a substitute for financial knowledge. Our "altars" are now similar to groves and monologue shrines where molten and carved images never talk to those who worship them. Only the priests dictate and feast on whatever the "oracle" demands. When God talks about financial prosperity, He talks in principles that don't depend on the mood of a preacher or the appetite of a smooth-talker. But when God talks protocols, we refuse to listen. Our "altars" are louder than our ledgers. Our pastor's demands are more revered than what God's principles demand.

We trust in oil, but not in order. We exalt pastors, but exclude God's principles. Their anointing for prosperity is richer in our estimations than our understanding of financial principles. We invest in their concerts, but not in our own capacity.

Try this simple test in any church:

- Ask how many believe in financial miracles, hands will shoot up everywhere.
- Ask how many understand the difference between the seed and the bread of their income, very few will stand, because these are either not taught or wrongly taught, though Scripture makes them plain.
- Then ask how many of those standing regularly separate their seed for sowing in their soil, the number will drop
- Lastly, ask how many have a real financial plan, beyond just hope and hustle, and you'll see the room go quiet.

Many believe in financial miracles, few understand seed and bread principle, and only a handful have a plan beyond hope and hustle in our congregations. Without following these changeless biblical principles, we will continue to transfer generational hardly-enough that breed exponential poverty in our assemblies.

God didn't design your financial miracle to depend on a mood in church; otherwise, those who are not easily swayed by emotional rhetoric would be confined to a financial cemetery. God didn't devise your financial future to depend on what the pastor says; else believers who have no access to pastors would be financially unfortunate. Rather, God wired financial miracles into simple and understandable laws, the laws of seed and bread, seedtime and harvest, and value exchange (or giving and receiving).

- No seed? No harvest.
- No planting? No progress.
- No giving? No gaining.

It's time to mature. Consuming your seed is at variance with how financial riches are built, even if you pray more fervently than Abraham and worship more exuberantly than David. You still need to go back and sow into your own field after your fervent prayer and exuberant worship.

It's time to dismantle the emotionalism masquerading as faith in our churches. It's time to confront the truth. We've shouted at closed heavens while holding back our seeds from touching the soil of investing. We've cried for wealth we didn't cultivate. We've prophesied over barren ground but refused to till it.

You want financial miracles? Start with your seed: not that which you give to your pastor, but a directed, intentional, sacrificial seed planted in your own field.

Give to the poor. Support kingdom missions. But you must invest in your own field. God never blesses empty hands that are lifted in worship, but tightened in giving and clenched in sowing.

Let the new declaration in our churches be:

"Pray, yes, but plant your seed."
"Worship, yes, but work the Word."
"Shout, yes, but save and sow, too."

Faith is not foolishness. Anointing is not arithmetic. Miracles do not override your reckless spending and perennial mismanagement. If you want those occasional, manna-like provisions, you may keep getting them, most folks do. But if you want to grow kingdom riches, you must obey the principles of seed and bread, sowing and reaping, giving and receiving.

Abraham didn't just build altars of worship. He sowed before reaping.

Isaac didn't just shout and laughed holy laughter. He planted before harvesting.

The widow didn't just give to a prophet. She sold oil to interested buyers to experience financial growth and change of fortune.

Despite being the king, David cultivated his land, engaging many farmers and farm managers. Read first Chronicles chapter twenty-seven with open minds. David had vineyards. He had a business that produced wine from the harvested fruit of the vine. He had olive groves. Another of his businesses produced olive oil from his olive yard. He built storehouses in several places. He raised cattle in different places, and I believe he developed the milk, the meat, and possibly the leather into some profit-generating enterprises as an example for whoever desires to follow the principles that made him such a multi-dimensional value creator. David had a dromedary where camels were raised. He reared donkeys. I'm not referring to the services he rendered while working for his father. David had his own goat farm as a king. He had his own sheep farming while he led his people.

Did he pray? Passionately! Did he worship God? Lavishly! But he also keyed into the principles that many folks prayerfully ignore while zealously "dancing like David danced."

The formula hasn't changed: Seed + Soil = Increased Supply

So, stop chasing financial deliverance like it's a lottery.

Start sowing like it's a lifestyle. Heaven doesn't release wealth to the loudest, it releases wealth to the wisest that diligently follows financial protocols.

And the seed in your hand might just be the key to the miracle you've been praying for all year.

Let it go (into your own soil).

Let it grow (in due course).

Let it multiply (through reproduction and duplication).

Let it compound (through exponential factors, adding new gains to the existing base) This is how financial miracles are born.

Prosperity is by Principles, Not by Supplication

Prayer works tremendously, and I have witnessed its undisputable results over the years. But prayer does not overrule biblical principles or become a substitute for the clearly written processes that guide wealth creation in the word of God. Have you ever seen anyone who became prosperous without offering a product or service, without creating, adding, or exchanging value? Ever seen success where no value was given, no hands got dirty, and no seed met soil? Is there true wealth without creation, without service, without exchange?

Lots of stories in the Bible teach us these same principles that many folks do prayerfully ignore today. The pattern is the same. The standard is sturdy, solid, and sure. The LORD God prospers individuals by readily commanding His blessings upon the products, services, and values we create, add to, or distribute. Kingdom riches never find the hands that never built, never sowed, never dared to trade value for value. You are not likely to be the defiant exception. No heir of salvation ever walks the road to prosperity, having never sown, never served, never broken ground, never lifted another, and never shaped a single gift for the world.

If you are not delivering value somewhere, your pastor's anointing cannot 'fall on' your $50 offering in order to produce enough dollars that will take care of your needs for the next one year! Without creating, adding, distributing, or recommending value, and strictly adhering to some other associated financial codes laid down in the word of God, no amount of laying-on of hands can convert your church attendance and activities into financial prosperity. Such activities could make you rich in spirit, and that's okay. But the scope of resources made available to kingdom citizens is not by any means limited to spiritual, if, with the right knowledge, you can comply with other scriptural principles.

Look intently at the Lord Jesus Christ. He obeyed biblical principles and also followed biblical processes. The protocols of the kingdom do not establish one as a substitute for the other. Biblical principles produce their results when correctly obeyed. Biblical processes produce their own results when thoroughly adhered to. And God is rich in results in the aspect of principles, without lacking resources in the aspect of processes. It is your foot-dragging that makes you choose the one and ignore the other—with results that are commensurate with your choices. You cannot prayerfully ignore biblical principles and expect God to offer you through praying, that which He established to be accessed by principles. This is the omission that lets some focus on Jesus's personality while neglecting

His principles and some others pay attention to His principles while ignoring His processes. Everyone gets the results of his or her choices.

The same principles that bring few folks who meet the requisite terms and conditions into a continuous flow of wealth and abundance also confine defiant and ignorant multitudes to a life of perpetual lack–even when some of them shadow more than disciples and supplicate more than Bartimaeus. Prosperity is on God's agenda for the redeemed. Notwithstanding, poverty readily befriends the redeemed who disregard ageless principles governing wealth creation and sustention. Against such, there is no therapy. Against such, there is no remedial anointing.

Shouting the loudest 'Amen' never precisely brings anyone out of poverty–without first sowing seeds that culminate in an exchange of value. It just doesn't make biblical sense. In fact, it contravenes biblical principles for anyone to grow riches by giving offering to some pastors and shouting 'the loudest amen' to "prophetic encounters", without contributing value elsewhere! Whose example would such be following? Who has ever built riches "in a godly manner" without offering something of value that you want to pattern your approach after?

Prayer without the exchange of value, whether offered personally or by men and women of 'heavy' anointing, doesn't make anyone wealthy. You may receive directions and instructions for necessary actions after praying. You may receive gifts, giftings, and graces through the laying on of hands, but you need to operate those gifts, giftings, and graces in order to create or add value. That's a starting point to operating in God's promised blessings—not in trickles but the kind that usher people into wealth creation and sustention. Value exchange is at the preliminary stage. Beyond exchange of value, there are specific, actionable principles that co-exist as a suit of financial codes which guide turning value into money, turning money into riches, and sustaining the flow of riches for a prolonged period. This is the focus of this book.

God established a changeless decree that keeps the oceans perpetually in their place, with no need for anyone to offer prayers to hold those massive bodies of water in their positions. Because there are immutable principles that govern the process of seed germination in a conducive environment, viable seeds will sprout with no need for prayer vigils. In the same vein, wealth creation is not to be accessed by prayers since God established ageless decrees which regulate it; so that just about anyone, regardless of race or creed, can gain the right of entry into abundance and financial freedom by following established principles. With those vastly potent, highly reliable principles already in place, the people who engage prayers as the only means for unlocking and accessing wealth creation and riches are possibly ignorant, possibly stubborn, or are bent on taking shortcuts with the LORD God who never circumvents His own terms.

If prayers alone bring people into prosperity, then imagine how prosperous some individuals and some nation-states would have become! But it doesn't. Something else does. Don't quit praying because it works tremendous works when rightly channelled. There are many things to pray for, but your prayers will only change you, not God's principles. Nobody flows into riches exclusively through prayers. Maybe you should pray to understand and properly follow the principles God established to power prosperity instead. Maybe you should pray that your heart and hands would be made ready to conform to prosperity's guiding principles.

There are kingdom benefits that are accessible through prayer, and there are those you can retrieve through principles. While prayer is a good catalyst, which indeed steadies and sometimes hastens the outcome of applied principles, its power weakens on the ignorance or stubbornness of those who adamantly insist on making it a substitute. Kingdom riches are attainable to kingdom citizens through kingdom principles clearly written in the Word of God.

Poverty Operates in Levels

Millions of folks don't look poor. That's possibly the reason many do not see how risky their situation has become. Their kids wear shoes. They post photos from birthday dinners. Their Instagram bio reads, "God first. Career second." They have stable jobs. Some even run their job-like businesses.

But pull back the curtain.

Go past the filter.

Turn the volume down on the worship music.

And you'll hear it: the silent hum of survival, the quiet torment of living on edge, the pressure of keeping up appearances while falling apart financially.

They are not beggars, but most are broke to the bone, and many are broken by debts.

There are levels to poverty, yes, layers, not labels. And while some wear mandarin-collar shirts, fit and flare dresses, and swipe cards, they're only a few salary cycles away from desperation. Poverty is not always the face on a begging mat or the child with a swollen belly. It can wear a suit. It can show up in offices, churches, and homes that seem beautiful on the outside. Sometimes, it's the polished manager in debt up to his collarbone. Sometimes, it's the faithful usher who tithes loyally but can't pay her rent on time. It can hide behind smiles, titles, and routines. Someone might look "put together" but still struggle with financial lack, emotional scarcity, or deep unmet needs.

Poverty is sneaky. Poverty isn't always loud or tattered. It wears perfume, types on a laptop, or leads morning meetings. It quotes Scripture and even shows up at conferences with a notepad. But peel back the layers, and you'll see it for what it is: a life quietly cracking under the pressure of "just enough," a wallet always behind, a tomorrow mortgaged for today's survival. This is not just about empty pockets. It's about exhausted souls. And to confront it, we must expose its levels, identify its patterns, and rip the mask off its many disguises.

1st Level: Barely Enough.

This is the gateway.

This is the first level of poverty, where income exists, but boundary doesn't.

It's polished. It speaks phonetics. It occupies an executive position and earns fat pay. It has a business license and pays taxes. But it is still poverty.

This is where most middle-class believers and citizens lodge. They have climbed out of the pit, but are still surrounded by walls. They live from contract to contract, from client to client. They make just enough to look stable, but not enough to stop grinding. They can rarely survive their lifestyle 6 months after their last contract or a layoff from their high-paying employment.

They can do without budgets and spend so carelessly. They can replace an expensive fridge without notice and without blinking. It is common for them to travel on exclusive vacation packages. They may even sponsor a cousin's wedding.

But they cannot rest, because they are still trapped in effort-based income.

If they don't show up, money doesn't either. If sickness hits, supply pauses. They have assets, but not systems. They have property, but not financial productivity. They have savings, but only because they're afraid, not free. They tithe and give, praise God. But they have no system of setting seed aside from bread.

These people are not rich; but they mimic the rich. Earning a fat salary doesn't make anyone rich. Winning a huge contract is not the same as being rich. It is what you do with your income that determines where you belong. Famous football players who played for top European Leagues and earned in a week what an experienced project manager earns in a year have been known to go broke and in debt a few years after their playing careers. They are typical examples of barely-enough, who grew the habits of spending according to the size of their income, not according to the size of their bread.

You are barely enough if you earn a million dollars per annum and spend a million dollars per annum: on toys, on luxury deals, on assets that lose value faster than they add it. You mistake current earning for personal worth. You muddle true worth with present public image. I assume you forgot, or possibly never understood, that even the Bible prototypes and demands separation of seed from bread. You have confused sowing with status maintenance.

I know you love God, sincerely. But you trust salary more than systems. Your fear of losing status is more than the dread of staying stagnant. You can host an impromptu team meeting in a fashionable suite. You invest in comfort, not in cash flow. So, you remain there: not in crisis, but in quiet captivity; not broke, but not free either.

2nd Level: Hardly Enough

The second level of poverty is even more dramatic. It has upper and lower classes.

Upper Class (Hardly Enough)

This is that level where everything earned is already owed; where salaries come in right now and disappear by nightfall.

The upper class of *Hardly Enough* are the ones who mistake cash flow for wealth. Who think because they get paid monthly, they are "okay." But if their job stopped for 90 days, so would their lives. One emergency, just one, and the entire house of cards would collapse.

They don't know they're poor, because they eat chicken on Sundays. They don't think they are poor because they send their kids to decent schools. They tithe. They lead prayer meetings. They own an iPhone and a data plan.

But in truth, they are a layoff away from hunger. They are a medical bill away from disaster. They are a car repair away from choosing between rent and food.

And you know the most dangerous of all? They call this normal. They baptize this bondage with the phrase: "At least we're managing."

No, you're not managing. You're bleeding quietly, steadily, devoutly.

Lower Class (Hardly Enough)

The lower class of *hardly enough* wears shame like cologne. It is visible, tangible, and loud. There is no hiding here. No Instagram filter can mask it.

It's the family sleeping in one room. It is the woman selling her wedding ring to pay school fees; the man ghosting friends because the landlord came again.

It's bounced cheques and borrowed dignity. It's the child sent home from school. It's the single mother skipping meals. It's the immigrant working three jobs and still behind on rent. And most tragically, it's the prayer warrior who thinks they're under generational curses when they're really just operating outside divine financial laws.

This level wears the soul thin. It humiliates. It chokes identity. It kills confidence. It makes church feel like a place of escape, but not a place of empowerment.

They love God, but they fear life. They have hope, but no tools. They are trapped in a theology of breakthroughs, but robbed of the discipline of building. They are inspired and sometimes cry during sermons. But the landlord still knocks. They donate during conventions, but the bank still calls.

3rd Level: Alleviated Poverty

This is not comfort. It is just a delay of collapse. It's not stability, but suspended survival.

This is the place where people live only because others let them. They're not paying rent because they don't have to.

They can't.

They're "managing" in a friend's basement. They stay quiet in their cousin's living room. They're an unspoken burden on someone else's overstretched grace.

Their food comes from the kindness of institutions: government cards, food banks, leftovers, and subsidies.

They don't remember the last time they bought groceries at full price, because that would mean not paying for transport.

They don't choose brands. They don't check for organic products. They just pick whatever is marked "free" or "on sale." Every meal is mercy. Every month is a miracle.

They don't live; they get carried. And though their bodies still move, their dignity often doesn't.

They laugh at church potlucks, but avoid eye contact during offerings. They say, "I'm in between jobs," but there is no job on the horizon.

They dress well, thanks to charity bins. If they post online, it is through borrowed Wi-Fi.

They live in waiting rooms: waiting for an email, waiting for a breakthrough, waiting for some kind of lifeline to stop the slow drown.

They smile to hide the pain. They "thank God" to mask the fatigue.

They don't complain because they know others have it worse. But deep down, they're tired of borrowing breath. This is not the middle ground. It's the edge.

It is a fragile place where a delayed promise or an expired benefit can mean sleeping on the street.

And still, they're told, "Don't worry. God will provide."

Yes. But God's provision is not designed to be an event. By principle, it's a system. And without the system, this level slowly swallows people whole.

4th Level: Aggravated Poverty

Here, the floor vanishes.

Here, poverty is not a level, it's a prison. It has no windows, no roof, and no exit.

This is where people do not eat every day because there is nothing to eat.

It is not because there is a delay in income, but because there is no income. It is not about low funds, but about no funds.

This is the street corner. This is the refugee camp. This is the makeshift shack under a collapsed flyover. This is the train station bench. This is the cardboard box between dumpsters. This is children scrounging for leftovers in garbage.

Here, you see mothers mixing water with sugar to quiet hunger cries. Here, you meet fathers who once had dreams now trading labour for coins, just to buy one piece of bread.

They sleep wherever night meets them: no locks, no walls, and no heat. Rain is an event. Winter is a sentence.

They wake up, not to plan the day, but to survive it. They don't look ahead. They can't. Hope is very expensive here.

There is no doctor; no dentist, no medication, not even for the fevers that threaten to take a child at night.

And school? That's a luxury. What about books? Not even an idea.

They are the invisible humans in disaster documentaries. They are the ones the world calls "IDPs" and forgets.

They weren't born without dreams, they were just swallowed by systems that never made room for them.

There are no birthdays here, no Christmas gifts, and no New Year plans. Just another 24 hours to dodge death.

This is not unemployment. This is dehumanization.

When everything collapses, this is what remains: a shell of life still moving, still breathing, but waiting for nothing.

And yet, even here, God sees. Even here, grace flickers. But you must not only pray for them, you must awaken to prevent this from being your children's future.

This level is not far. It's just a few unchecked decisions away from the average earner.

Just a missed salary could be the beginning that pulls out the floor under your feet. Just a prolonged illness could turn night's dream into a nightmare. Just a life event with no backup plan could be the end of what used to be and the beginning of the inconceivable.

So, embrace the principles that guide others in creating riches from where they are. This is because no one intends to end up here, but many do, just by doing nothing, just by consuming their seed.

The Invisible Bondage of Paycheck Faithfuls

The lie is that only those who beg are poor. That only those who look unkempt or sleep under bridges need financial healing.

No!

Poverty is stealthy. It has PhDs. It attends midweek services. It sings alto in the choir. It wears heels and three-piece suits. Poverty sometimes smiles at baby dedications and comes back home to cry in the bathroom afterward. It gives testimonies of favour, and then borrows transport home.

Poverty isn't just a condition. It's a mindset. It's a mindset that says "I'm getting paid next week; so let's consume all we can today." It's a belief that says, "I earn well; therefore I'm fine."

But earning is not enough. Because the day the income stops, your true level shows. And if you have no seed stored, no system sown, you find out too late that you were never fine. You were just distracted. You were just deceived.

God never designed His people to live from hand to mouth. He never intended for us to eat everything we earn. He gave bread and seed. One is for consumption. The other is for continuation. The pathway to financial redemption is not just prayer, it is planting. It is not just giving, but growing; not just sowing emotionally, but sowing strategically.

If every income you get goes from salary to supermarket, from alert to airtime, from pay to panic, you are consuming your seed. You are eating your future.

The eaters bury their talents, the consumers waste their seed. The law of multiplication and increase was never designed to reward defiant eaters or favour disobedient consumers.

Only investors.
Only builders.
Only seeders.

To avoid Level Four takes wisdom, and sometimes war.
To rise beyond Levels Three and Two requires intentionality.
To remain at Level One is a choice, because you can move higher.

My call to you is simple, but stern. Break the cycle. Separate your seeds from your bread. Stop baptizing financial mismanagement with religious vocabulary. Start investing, not just in heaven, but in habits. This is because heaven responds not just to tears, but to truth.

And the truth is this: Many believers are broke, not because God didn't bless them, but because they mismanaged what He blessed them with.

You don't fix poverty with passion. You fix it with principles. Don't just pray for a breakthrough, but plant for continuity. Tithe, yes, but also build. Sow into retreats and conferences, but don't forget to store. Give to the poor, but don't become one in the process.

Stop eating all your income. That's not humility. That's harvest abuse.

This book is not a court verdict. This is a rescue call. This is a line thrown into deep waters for the drowning faithful.

God didn't call you to survive. He called you to steward, to overflow, to multiply.

Identify your level, then fight to arise.

You're not poor because you don't have money. You're poor when you don't have a system. You don't become wealthy because you have cash. You become wealthy when your seed has structure and your structure has vision.

So, I want to teach you to follow proven protocols: to identify and separate your seed; to sow it with wisdom; to build kingdom riches with intention; and to break up with hardly enough and searing poverty.

Chapter 6

God's Funnels of Provision

If you truly acknowledge God as your provider, then brace yourself for this truth: every provision of God contains seed and bread. He never sends bread alone. He never sends seed alone. He sends both, always both. Every time God dispenses provision to humankind, it comes as a lump quantity of seed and bread. Every provision that flows from His hand carries this dual nature: seed for the future, bread for now. It's never just lunch. It's a package coded with tomorrow's harvest, encrypted inside today's meal. How wonderful is our God, who, whenever He provides for anyone at any of the three layers, delivers it in this same format of seed and bread: seed for sowing, bread for food! That has been an age-long code ingrained in the principles of provision, waiting to be deciphered by anyone who wishes to maximize the layers of God's provision. It's how He works.

This principle does not bend, regardless of your acceptance or rejection of being governed by it. As a matter of fact, the principle does not bow, irrespective of the pressure of hunger and lack at the home front or the burden of starvation at the community level.

When He supplies, He doesn't merely answer your needs; He embeds a strategy in the surplus. Whether you're at the first layer of scraping by, the second of sustaining, or the third of surplus, the protocol is the same: seed and bread. Misread it, and you'll eat what should have been sown. Ignore it, and your tomorrow becomes a desert shaped by today's indulgence. The principle does not sympathize. It doesn't shrink for pity. It stands unbending: through hunger, through hardship, through cries from empty kitchens and dry storehouses. Accept it or not, the code governs the outcomes. It always has. It always will, as long as the earth endures.

This principle did not just surface in the New Testament. It has been from Genesis, and we will look at it more closely from the beginning. But for now, see what the Old Testament said in the days of Isaiah:

> For as the rain comes down, and the snow from heaven, and do not return there, but water the earth, and make it bring forth and bud, that it may give seed to the sower, and bread to the eater: Isaiah 55:10 (NKJV)

This is the same principle as is in the New Testament. Every fruit you've ever seen, be it juicy or dry, sweet or bitter, it contains this same coded message in plain sight: seed and bread. Every one of them comes split between this sacred truth: food and future. There's the edible flesh for today. And nestled within or beneath it, there's the seed for tomorrow.

Sometimes, you are to eat the fleshy, edible part and plant the seed portion. Sometimes you eat part of the harvest of fruits or grain and plant the rest. For pineapples, you eat the fruit and plant the sucker. For cassava, it could be the tuber you eat, and the stem you plant. For cassava, it could be a portion for dinner and another for the ground. This ancient rhythm hasn't changed. And it never will, as long as your supplies still bear the watermark of divinity, not the stain of fraud, manipulation, or crime.

Tragically, too many believers only recognize the bread, not the seed. They receive a harvest, feast on the whole portion, and shout, "God is good," until famine arrives like a thief. The same God who sends rain to water the earth also designed that the earth only responds to what is sown. Rain has its job. Soil has its duty. The seed has its purpose. The yield of seed and bread has its unique responsibility as well. But in sheer ignorance or outright defiance, we eat the bread, divert the seed, and consume every instalment of provision intended for both present sustenance and future forest.

Yet, until seed meets soil, nothing breaks forth. Ignorance, not Satan, is why many Christians are stuck in cycles of 'earn and exhaust'. They consume their seeds in the name of survival. They chew the entire portion, and wonder why nothing is multiplying. God never intended for His children to be full-time eaters. His original blueprint was clear: the eater must also be a sower. Anything less is a malfunction of purpose.

Every salary, every allowance, every profit, every wage, whatever name the container bears, is merely the shell. The content is what counts. The container may not indicate the composition, but the content is never mistaken in the standing order of God's prosperity protocol. And the content, in God's holy economics, is never just breakfast. It's composition. The label may not carry 'how to administer' description, but the content never loses the essence of its assignment in the originating principle of God's provision. The lane on which you set your feet, on the voyage of poverty or prosperity, begins at this crucial junction, where it is necessary to see the two components in your supplies and distinguish them appropriately. Bread is for the eater. Seed is for the sower. It's not a poetic metaphor; it's a governing principle. So, when next you see your payslip or contract earnings, don't just see money. See a sacred instruction hidden in the figure; a divine test disguised as digits; a spiritual assignment dressed up as a transfer alert.

Yes, I hear you. "But my income is barely enough!" Still, there is seed. "My profit is too small to share!" Still, there is seed. "My salary can't even cover rent!" Still, there is seed. Shoulder this truth and discover the corresponding lane to prosperity without inducement. Reject it and proceed along the corresponding pathway to poverty willy-nilly. If all you ever receive from God comes as bread, someone somewhere planted the seed that made your harvest possible. And you, yes, you, become a consumer of another man's obedience. That is not sustainable, being a perpetual eater. That is not spiritual maturity. That is not dominion.

Many of the things you can do if your income seems little or is actually inadequate were introduced in the previous chapter. You don't need millions to obey this law. What you need is light. And what this light reveals is sobering: the principle will not break just because you are broke. It will not pause simply because you are under pressure. It will not adjust its posture because you're overwhelmed. It will only wait until you obey it.

According to Isaiah, God 'gives seed to the sower and bread to the eater'. The two get supplied together, not one in January and the other in June. And, according to Paul, God 'ministers seed to the sower and bread for your food'. Both are administered concurrently, not one in winter and the other in summer.

God's provision comes as a lump. It is a fusion of nourishment and potential. And He expects you to discern it, divide it, and dispense it in alignment with His unfailing principle. Bread is for now. Seed is for what's next. If you eat both, you feast briefly and famish soon after. But if you eat the bread and sow the seed either back into the endeavour that generated it or in some other fields or ventures, you have partnered with heaven's code for increase.

This is not financial advice. This is a kingdom revelation. And it is the protocol by which believers rise above cycles. God's provision is administered by principle, and must be received and dispensed by principle. It is God's responsibility to provide for you as a chunk, but it is your responsibility to receive it as is, separate the seed from the bread, and then allot the proceeds as an obligatory stipulation by the standing principles of seed and bread. So, don't just earn. Don't just eat. Don't just survive. Distribute. Sow. Reinvest. And watch your tiny package multiply in ways you can't pray your way into, because you finally obeyed the protocol you once shouted over.

The funnel below is a depiction of God's funnel of provision at the first layer.

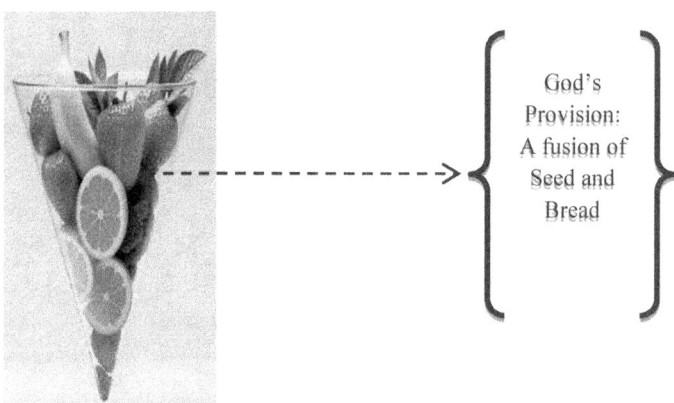

God's provision is a fusion of seed and bread

What Denotes Bread in God's Provision?

Bread is that part of your supply that you expend on any category of non-income generating expenditures. They could be food, clothing, gadgets, utilities, leisure, non-income generating subscriptions, personal residence, non-income generating rent, and such like.

What Denotes Seed in God's Provision?

Seed is that part of your supply that you expend on any category of income generating expenditures like training and development, business ventures, investments, income-generating real estate, intellectual properties, and such like.

Don't confuse your seed with your tithe. Don't mistake it for offering, even when a preacher declares, "Sow a seed" on the pulpit. And certainly, don't wrap it in charity and call it sowing. Each of those has its own spiritual lane, its own principle, its own protocol, and none should be hijacked to do the work of another. Your tithe is covenant; your offering is honour; your giving to the poor is mercy; but your seed, that sacred portion, is for sowing into your own field, not someone else's assignment. You don't sow your seed into your pastor's pocket or your prophet's prayer bowl. That may bring you favour, a thank-you note, or even open certain doors, but it won't produce a harvest in your field that is devoid of value exchange. Your sown seed must enter the soil of your own labour, your own field, your own God-given ground.

When you give to people, you may gain goodwill, access, connections, or even advice. But when you sow into your field, you secure a harvest of an incomparable kind, pressed down, shaken together, and running over, by divine law. Both giving and sowing are acts of release, but their goals are different, their scopes distinct, and their outcomes completely different.

God's Responsibility at the Layer of Basic Supply

God never fumbles with His end of the deal. He ministers provision, faithfully, constantly, deliberately. Like clockwork, He delivers your basic supplies in parcels marked with your current level of operation. If you're employed, He channels it through salaries, allowances, overtime bonuses, and incentives, tailored to your rank, your diligence, your growing excellence, and even your knack for spotting and seizing rare opportunities. If you've advanced to managerial lanes, royalty brackets, entrepreneurial corridors, or investor territories, your provisions shift into higher gears; often flowing in folds, double and triple, commensurate with your widening influence and multiplied impact.

But don't be distracted by the packaging. Whether the label reads "wage," "profit," "returns," "commission," "royalty," or "dividends," the content remains divine and coded: seed to be sown, bread to be eaten.

Every divine delivery carries both. It's your sacred duty to discern them. He provides. You divide. That's the principle. That's the protocol. And that's where most destinies are either made or marred.

God's Responsibilities at the Layer of Multiplication

God never designed basic supplies to be the end. Layer 1 was never the final act, just the first movement in a craft of increase. But He also won't strong-arm you into abundance. That's not His style. Instead, He embedded principles, clear, unwavering, inviolable, so that His ministration of supply would be matched by your wise administration of it. He gives. You administer. That's the deal. And governing begins with this sacred art: discerning the seed from the bread. If He intended you to consume it all, there'd be no seed in the package. But He doesn't just hand you bread; He tucks in seed, because multiplication is His next goal. And multiplication doesn't happen by magic. It happens by math. Real math! Seed math!

Multiplication is iterated addition. One number is repeatedly added to itself a certain number of times. The number being multiplied is called the multiplicand, while the number of times it is repeated is known as the multiplier. For example, three seeds sown four times don't mystically become a forest, it's 3 + 3 + 3 + 3. Simple, powerful, exact: 12.

When you don't separate (and sow) your seed from layer 1, there is nothing to multiply for you in this layer of multiplication. Using the above multiplication example, zero seed, multiplied a thousand times, is still zero. You get zero results even if God wants to multiply your seed 4 times. God does not multiply intentions. He multiplies action.

By this principle, God multiplies the seed that a man separates and sows. He is not bound to increase the seed you hoard, misplace, or divert. He doesn't multiply potential. He multiplies sown seed. Only what leaves your hand as a planter, returns to your life as a harvest.

God's Responsibility at the Layer of Increase

God longs to do far more for you than simply multiply what you've sown. But His longing does not override His laws. His mercy won't violate His method. His power won't cancel your part. He honours His word above desire, even His own. And while His heart beats with intention to elevate you, He won't bypass your obedience. His protocol stands: no increase without process, no overflow without order.

What He offers at the third layer, the layer of divine increase, makes the second layer's multiplication look like child's play. While multiplication is repeated addition, increase is compounded essence, growth in exponential dimensions. The difference in scope and result are mind-boggling.

This is where a seed morphs into a forest. One book becomes a collection translated into various languages. A single branch gives rise to a flourishing grove. A product gains legs, then wings, then nations. One service stretches into a franchise that spills over continents. A song matures into a symphony of albums echoing through distant homes. A short film evolves into a cinematic universe. A startup transforms into a multinational. A simple label rises to the weight of a global brand. That's not mere growth, it's divine acceleration. This is what happens when God breathes on what you dared to sow.

God's Responsibilities across the 3 Layers

By these unbending principles, God ministers to each person according to the boundaries of their obedience. One may receive only at the layer of basic supply, because that's where their compliance begins, and ends. Another, standing under the same heaven, may receive at all three layers, basic supply, multiplication, and increase, not

God's Funnel of provision across the 3 layers

because God has favourites, but because He honours principles, not pity. It is not divine limitation. It is human calibration. God is not withholding; it is man who is not complying. You don't get what He wants to give; you get what you're positioned to receive. In due course, it is not God, but you who determine the measure of your portion.

The diagram on the left is a simple depiction of God's responsibilities in providing for His own across the three layers of provision.

First Leg (Layer of Basic Supply):

This is the entry-level layer of divine provision where God sends supplies in the form of salaries, allowances, commissions, profits, bonuses, inheritances, awards, and even raffle wins. Yes, God sends them. But tragically, this is the same layer where most believers imprison His hand. They freeze God's economy at this base level, by their own doing. Why? Because they refuse to discern the anatomy of divine supply. They never separate the seeds from the bread. They eat everything: every cent, every dollar, every allowance, like entitled consumers, not conscious stewards.

Layer of Basic Supply

Some parade new cars. Some take selfies in exotic destinations. Some sip cocktails by the beach, calling it "God's blessings." But the façade cracks quickly. Give them six months of job loss, sickness, a market crash, or early retirement, and the truth begins to gnaw. Their poverty doesn't start then. It was only unmasked.

Hear this again, loud and clear: the surest path to poverty is consuming your entire income. Fast cars and expensive perfume don't disguise financial foolishness for long. Poverty isn't just a matter of what you earn; it's what you retain, what you sow, and what you build. And if you're stuck in this layer, it's because of some chronic ignorance, stubborn defiance, or an undisciplined appetite; all fully authorized by your own approval stamp.

God is not under pressure to break His own principles for anyone, not even you. He sends basic supplies, yes. But He waits. He watches. He looks for obedience. Because the same God who gives bread, gives seed. And the supply doesn't move to multiplication or increase unless you honour the principle. That law is ancient. It is ageless. And it works in every nation, industry, or field, without bias, without partiality.

Second Leg (Layer of Multiplication):

There is a standing decree at this second layer, ancient, active, and unbending, that multiplies sown seed: not when it is admired, not when it is hoarded, not even when it is separated, but when it is sown. It multiplies seed when it is sown rightly, in the right soil, under the right heart posture. This divine protocol is not hindered by geography; it works in the boardrooms of Manhattan and in the backyards of Makoko.

Layer of Multiplication

The rural village and the bustling city are both within range of its activation. Bravo to those who've discerned their seed portion and resisted the urge to consume it. Bravo to those who no longer confuse seed for bread. These are not just waiting on God; they're walking with Him. Those seeds are destined to multiplication in this second leg, with the sowers assured of receiving supplies at both the first leg and multiples of what is sown at the second leg.

Seed separation is therefore like your map reading, while seed sowing is like the actual commencement of this exciting voyage. These two components are essential stepping stones that begin the exciting journey. That's when the real journey begins.

It's a journey paved with covenant and laced with promise. God doesn't merely cheer you on; He powers the multiplication. Every sown seed is a transaction with eternity. The more you sow, the more heaven has permission to multiply.

The terrain won't always be smooth. There'll be steep climbs and stony paths. The weather may change, and the ground may groan. But don't misread the difficulty for denial. The path of sowing isn't designed for convenience, it's designed for consequence. The detours of delay may tempt you to turn back. The temptation to consume what was meant to be sown may scream at your belly. But make no mistake; this is still the road to wealth. This is still the route to lasting riches. The seed may fall with trembling, but it rises for sure in multiplied triumph.

Third Leg (Layer of Increase):

Here, God increases your blessings in exponential powers, compounding every component in rounds upon rounds of increase. Here, the laws of arithmetic give way to the mystery of the exponential. This is not mere multiplication; it is the more radical, more potent compounding increase, where every layer of blessing rides on the shoulders of the last, gaining momentum like waves that deepen as they roll.

Here, God doesn't just add to your storehouse, He amplifies. He doesn't just multiply your harvest, He folds it over in cycles and seasons, pressing it down, shaking it together, and making it run over with terrifying beauty. The blessing at this layer is not a trickle, it's a torrent. Not a paycheck, it's a pattern. It builds, swells, and compounds until your baskets tremble under divine surplus.

Blessed are those who are tenacious till this point in the voyage, sowing their multiplied seed (from Layer 2) rather than increasing their consumption with extravagant living; for they shall secure deliveries at the basic, the multiplication and the amplified layers of God's provision.

Layer of Increase

Blessed, yes, significantly blessed, are the ones who've walked through the furnace of delay without scorching their seed in indulgence. Those who chose to sow again rather than squander their gains from multiplication. These are the fortunate voyagers who refuse to inflate their lifestyle with every increase, who reject the temptation to make consumption their god. To them is given access to the triple-fold layers of divine provision: the portion of daily supply, the harvest of multiplied seed, and the thunderous flood of exponential increase. This is no longer survival; it's no longer seasonal abundance. This is the dimension of legacy.

Your Choices determine your Outcome

By the same divine principles that govern God's provision, one man can live dutifully for decades on wages, earnings, and allowances, scraping value from his skills like a miner digging through sand. He works, earns, spends, and repeats, then leans heavily on a retirement savings plan as if it were a ventilator, hoping it holds out longer than his breath. Another, wiser in the principles, earns a salary too, but adds ventures to his arsenal, builds small investment nests, and secures a future where money still works even when he can't. Then, there's yet another, walking the higher paths of kingdom principle, whose life is a cascade of abundance. Chains of businesses hum with activity beneath his oversight. Investment portfolios drip continuous yields. Royalties stream in from past labours, from books, patents, products, songs, systems, proof that he sowed with precision and obeyed without shortcuts. Even in his sleep, value answers to him. Even in death, his wealth outlives him.

It is God's faithfulness to minister to each according to the layers they've chosen. He is no respecter of titles, but of principles. Whether you approve your confinement to the consumer lane of layer 1, with careless defiance, or you gain access to deeper layers through rugged compliance, God remains faithful. But He is never wasteful. He does not distribute the rewards of Layer 3 to those stuck in the syndrome of Layer 1. He cannot be lured into violating His own laws. Nor is He unjust to disburse only Layer 1 results to a man who labours diligently in Layers 2 and 3, building engines of value and rivers of impact. Your reality is not a prophecy; it is a principle. Your portion is not random; it is rooted. Your result is not a mystery; it is the exact harvest of your chosen actions and applied truths. In a growing kingdom, riches don't lie; they only echo your decisions.

Evolution of Your Seed

Now, let's read that verse again and observe the illustrative diagram.

Now he that soweth seed to the sower both minister bread for your food, and multiply your seed sown, and increase the fruits of your righteousness.

The seed portion of your supply was never designed to die in layer 1. It was sculpted by divine order to journey, layer upon layer, until it matures into a kind of prosperity that time cannot erase and death cannot silence. But alas, most never taste this kingdom reality. Why? Because their seeds never travel beyond the first gate of God's provision. They hoard it. They eat it. They bury it under fear, impulse, and short-sightedness. And by so doing, they sentence themselves to the congested, frustrating traffic jam of "never enough;" where dreams age and wealth decay. But the one who dares to release his seed, who lets it sail beyond layer one, endure the fires of multiplication in layer two, and embrace the mystery of increase in layer three, he boards the road less travelled; the path to super-abundance, the highway to wealth that outlives breath, the lane where legacy overtakes lack.

And no, beloved, shouting the loudest "hallelujah" won't change your lane. You can sob in tongues, roll on the carpet, give prophetic handshakes to strangers, yet none of it overrides this ageless principle. No "new move of God" can overwrite this enduring law, written in the archives of the Kingdom's economy, in order to bring you into a different outcome than the choices you make with the seed portion of your income.

You may stumble into wealth by favour, windfall, or wonder, but if your seed is not separated and sown, your story will still collapse in the same predictable ruin. You may receive $1 Million cash gift today, win $10 Million lottery in a month's time, and receive $100 Million in annual wages as is common in some popular sports, you may end up settling on the pathway to poverty when you consume everything without separating and sowing the seed portion of your rewards into some income generating ventures.

That's why statistics expose a brutal irony: 70% of lottery winners end up broke and a third go on to declare bankruptcy. Many, once kissed by millions, now beg for thousands. That's why ex-athletes and high-profile sports persons, who once touched millions weekly, chartered private jets at will, and purchased luxury cars like toys, fade into shadows of bankruptcy once the cheering stops. Not because money failed, but because principle was violated. The voyager's boat docks not where he wishes, but where its takers and the tide authorize the vessel of his seed to anchor. Your outcomes are not governed by emotion, anointing, or ambition; they are governed by where your seed is planted, how far it travels, and the protocol it submits to. Your supply answers only to the legitimate provisions of the layer your seed qualifies for: nothing more, nothing less.

Chapter 7

Man's Funnel of Receiving

Though God releases supplies by the unshakable laws of divine provision, man must not handle it with casual hands or untrained hearts. Every heaven-sent supply must be received under two sacred protocols: first, with the bowed head of gratitude; and second, with the discerning hands that separate what is to be sown from what is to be eaten. Gratitude opens the gate. Discernment sets the order. For without thanksgiving, the supply is mishandled; and without separation, the seed is lost in the breadbasket of consumption.

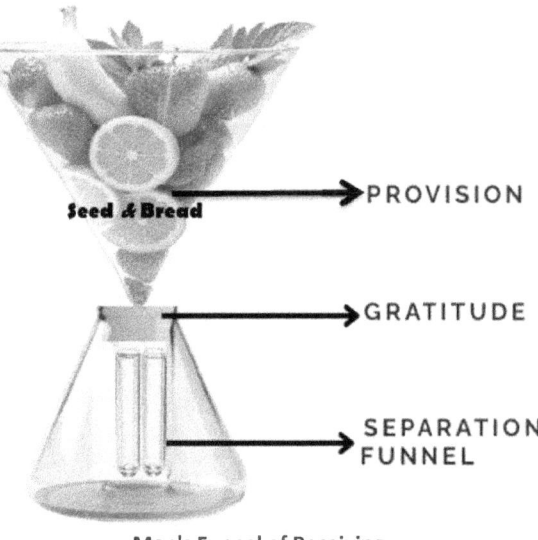

Man's Funnel of Receiving

As far as heaven's ledger reads, God never defaults on His side of provision. The fault lines, as always, run on our side. He faithfully sends the parcel, dependably containing "seed and bread." But we mishandle the contents too often. Either we tear it open with entitlement, void of gratitude, or we swallow it whole without discernment.

Let me ask plainly: when last did you lift your voice in thanksgiving after your salary dropped? Do you whisper gratitude when profits roll in from your shop, your hustle, your gig? Or have you grown so used to the rhythm of receipts that you now see wages as the trophy of your sweat, not the trust of His supply? That's where the leak begins. That's where failure silently sets in; when provision is mistaken for payment, and we forget that grace authored both the work and the wage.

There are countless believers who have never once seen their monthly salary as divine supply. When the contract is signed, they nod to their competence. When bonuses hit, they toast to their brilliance. But heaven watches, grieved; not because you earn, but because you forget who enabled the earning. And worse still, because you consume every increase as if it were all seedless.

Friend, hear this: every godly provision, no matter how it arrives, is to be received with reverence, not routine; and with gratitude, not greed. And once received, it must be separated accordingly: bread for your present nourishment, and seed for your future multiplication. Bonus is not a bread-only parcel. Profit is not seed-exempt. To treat them as such is to trample on the protocol of God's prosperity; and to choose, knowingly or not, the path of lack in the midst of plenty.

Man's Responsibility in Receiving Supplies

The moment God releases supply, He steps back, not in absence, but in expectation. He has done His part, true to covenant. The parcel arrives, with seed wrapped in bread, sustenance stitched into potential. But that's only the first turn on the tri-leg voyage. The curtain lifts, but the plot isn't finished.

And now, He waits, not passively, but purposefully. He waits, not because He's uncertain, but because the principle He authored demands your next move. Will you recognize the seed? Will you separate with reverence? Will you sow or will you swallow it whole?

God stands ready, sleeves rolled, to release the next layer, loaded with multiplication. And He waits again to unveil the third: the exponential. But both are governed by the same principles He etched into the fabric of increase. He is the Giver. But you, dear steward, are the governor of your own outcomes. He is faithful to supply the seed and the bread, but He will not break His own principles to force a harvest you have not authorized.

Look at that verse again:

> **Now he that ministereth seed to the sower both minister bread for your food, and multiply your seed sown, and increase the fruits of your righteousness.** 2 Cor 9:10 (KJV)

The significance of the bread ends the moment it's consumed as your food. Your bread from one layer has no business in the next layer because its assignment carries a term limit. Its journey is brief. It serves you momentarily. It does not graduate into tomorrow because tomorrow has another instalment in waiting. It fills the belly, fuels the feet, but fades with the setting sun. Bread belongs to the now, not the next. Its assignment is seasonal; its value valid only within its window. So eat it. Share it. Save it for a while if you must. There is no law against such. But never hoard it for permanence, because the next portion is coming shortly with its own distinctive bread.

Is bread therefore significant? Yes, bread is sacred. It is heaven's kindness wrapped in calories. It keeps your bones from breaking, your mind from fainting. It nourishes the body and meets immediate needs. But it has no power to multiply itself. It is the grace for survival, not the guarantee of increase. And for those whose eyes see only bread in every package, poverty is merely a matter of time. God, in His wisdom, hides the architecture of abundance not in the size of your paycheck, but in the supplemented presence of a seed. He buries tomorrow's orchard inside today's overlooked kernel. Only those who learn to discern, to separate, and to sow can cross over from survival to surplus, from addition to multiplication, from layer 1 to layer

Bread is very useful. Bread is very instrumental if you must oil the wheels of life. But, of what significance is life if the only thing is to oil its wheels without heading to its destination? Bread is vital, but life is more than bread. Bread is fuel for the voyage, not the voyage itself. You weren't born to chase after bakeries. You were born to build barns. There must be more to your journey than the scent of daily loaves. No wise man buys gas just to burn gas. No sane pilgrim starts a journey just to consume the engine's oil. Yet, many have turned their entire lives into sophisticated bread-eating operations. What a tragedy to keep consuming and never advancing! What pain to own resources and squander destiny!

And the seed? Ah, the seed is a distinct entity entirely. It is time, compressed. It is abundance disguised. It is wealth in hiding. It is the covenant material God uses to unfold your future. But when you eat your seed, you chew up tomorrow's forest to light today's matchstick. You abort all conceivable multiplication before it breathes. You terminate all inconceivable exponential increases before they take root. Seed is not a donation. It is not a tithe. It is not a goodwill gesture to your pastor or a random act of kindness to the poor. Those things have their rewards. But seed must enter a field, your field. It must find soil. It must die. Only then can it multiply.

God *'ministers seed to the sower'*, and blesses or *'multiplies your seed sown'*, and *'increases the fruit....'* And when that ministered seed becomes sown seed, He multiplies it. And after multiplication, He increases the seed base with the seed gain, exponentially, not arithmetically. But note this: It is not the seed received that gets multiplied, but the seed sown. It is not the seed kept that becomes fruit, but the seed buried. If your seed never leaves your hand, your harvest will never leave the realm of imagination.

These are not emotional thoughts. These are not theological musings. These are principles, unchanging, immovable, and timeless. And the moment you receive your provision, God steps back, not to abandon you, but to see what you will do with what He has given. He has already loaded the parcel with bread and seed. He won't repeat Himself. The rest is your move.

What happens if seed is not separated? It's erroneously eaten as if it were bread, and there is nothing left to complete the remaining two legs.

Without sown seed, there is really nothing for God to bless with sprouts and blossoms in the second leg of that principle. And where blossom is absent, fruiting is a mere dream. Where there is no sown seed, the instalment of provision gets pegged to the first layer of God's provision, where there is only your basic, regular, and measured supply; and nothing more.

This is the reason some stay at Layer 1 for a lifetime: surviving, earning, consuming, but never ascending. They receive and eat; again, and again, and again. But others, those who separate, those who sow, step into Layer 2, where multiplication beckons. And when they persist, stewarding multiplied seed with discipline, they ascend into Layer 3, where increase arrives in exponential compounds: more than imagined, more than deserved, more than earned.

And so I ask you: how long will you keep mistaking seed for bread? How long will you silence your future to satisfy your today? There is more, much more, in the hands of God, but He waits. Not at the gates of heaven, but at the next layer of principle. Will your seed ever arrive there? Or will it die on the tongue of momentary appetite?

Your seed is not optional. It is your covenant with tomorrow.

So, take time to look at that scripture again.

> **Now he that ministereth seed to the sower both minister bread for your food, and multiply your seed sown, and increase the fruits of your righteousness.** 2 Cor 9:10 (KJV)

Observe the following implications:

a. God is intricately involved in all three layers of provision: the layer of supply, the layer of multiplication, and the layer of increase. But He does not walk these layers alone. Man, too, is called into active partnership, responsible, discerning, and diligent, within these same layers. It is a divine collaboration where God initiates the process and calls the man to reciprocate in obedience.

b. Between the ministered seed and the sown seed lies a sacred interval: unspoken, invisible, yet loaded with consequence. Scripture clothes it in a simple word: "**and**." But this "and" is no casual conjunction; it is a loaded pause, heavy with responsibility. For in that silence, God waits, not to act, but to see if the recipient will discern, separate, and sow.
c. There is yet another divine pause, masked again with the simplicity of the word "**and**," between multiplied seed and increased fruits. It is within this space that the sower is summoned once more: not just to harvest, but to steward. To recognize that within every multiplied return, there is a fresh portion of seed. And once again, the duty falls to the wise: to separate the bread for food and the seed for sowing, that the seed may journey further into the mystery of increase.
d. Each of these silent intervals is a divine handover point. God does not skip His part; neither should you. Your task is weighty and layered: to receive gratefully, separate wisely, store deliberately, sow purposefully, and tend faithfully. The soil will not plough itself. The vineyard will not water itself. But if you show up, heart in hand, tools in grip, then your fields will bloom, your harvests will cluster, and your barns will remember abundance.
e. A wise eater graduates into a sower, understanding that eating alone is not the endgame of provision. But a foolish eater, driven by appetite and dulled by short-sightedness, devours every

portion, leaving no seed to plant, no harvest to anticipate, and no altar upon which God's multiplying power can work.

f. God is not committed to multiplying bread. Bread is for consumption. Bread completes its voyage just beyond the mouth. It ends where the hunger ends. It is the seed alone that carries the genetic code of tomorrow. And God multiplies only what carries that code.

g. God commits only to multiplying the seed, and not the bread. The bread simply reaches the last lap of its voyage after each leg of these multi-sided principles.

h. God commits to the cycle of the seed, not the sweetness of the bread. Bread, no matter how delicious, is not designed to return. It is the seed, separated and stewarded and sown, that returns in waves and seasons. God it the Lord over layered increase, not layered consumption. And until a man understands this, he will walk cycles around provision, never entering the pathways of prosperity.

i. God commits to multiplying only **the seed that is sown**, nothing else carries that promise.

   i. Not the bread, because its voyage comes to an end at the table of nourishment.

   ii. Not the seed that is eaten as or with bread: whether in stubborn ignorance or subtle compromise.

   iii. Not the seed that is properly separated, yet casually consumed later. Regardless of your reasons, emergency, fear, pressure, or pain, the moment you devour your seed, you sabotage your destiny of multiplication. In kingdom economics, delayed sowing is not an excuse for justified eating.

iv. Not the seed that is separated but neglected, lost, or left to rot. This is a parable of waste: a treasure cast to swine, left exposed to moths, to rust, or to thieves. Heaven does not multiply what man mismanages or abandons.

v. Not the seed that is wisely separated, carefully preserved, yet never sown. A seed that sleeps in safes and vaults may be safe, but it remains sterile. For unless a grain falls to the ground and dies, it abides alone. And what abides alone remains unimpressive in eternity's ledger.

The weight of these truths places a solemn, non-transferable responsibility upon your shoulders, which you cannot afford to treat with levity or casual neglect. For with every fresh arrival of God's provision, day after day, month after month, you are not merely a receiver, but a steward summoned to discernment, distinction, and dutiful administration. You must not mishandle what Heaven has faithfully ministered.

What Happens if the Seed Is NOT Separated?

Whoever chooses to sidestep this pearl-principle of divine provision signs up, knowingly or not, for the risk of scarcity, the sting of poverty, and the haunting echo of dreams that never took flight. It is not a curse; it is simply the consequence of neglect. When the whole of your provision is consumed as bread, you sound the alarm that halts the train of future supply. You peg your destiny to the borders of the basic supplies and compensatory tokens: salaries, wages, bonuses, allowances, overtime pays, and simple profits. You become stuck in the shallows of God's abundance, sipping from puddles when rivers await.

Yes, it feels good to spend it all at once, to quiet every hunger hastily, to meet every nagging need now. But therein lays the quiet sabotage of destiny. Because to treat all you receive as bread is to declare your portion finished. It is to bury the potential of your seed beneath today's appetite. And every time your seed dies in your mouth rather than in the soil, you delay your harvest; you abort your multiplication; you exile your increase. Such actions could be ideal for your bread, but it's a disservice to your seed. It triggers the shutdown of tomorrow's multiplication and activates a blackout to future increase. It keeps you stuck at the entry level of provision and limits what God can do through you and for you.

The harsh truth is this: when all your money goes to survival, you disconnect from revival. When you consume the whole, you cancel the miracle housed in your seed, the one God sent to unlock extra dimensions of favour, creativity, access, innovation, and multiplication. You doom yourself to an endless cycle of just-enough, living on repeat, from paycheck to pressure, from deposit to depletion. And while God stands ready to release more, the door remains bolted from your end: sealed by your own hands that sowed nothing.

So, here's the sober question ringing through eternity: Will you reduce the fullness of God's supply to the limits of your pocket? Will you confine heaven's intention to what your hand can consume? Or will you rise, separate the seed, honour the bread, and journey beyond the veil into the layers where God multiplies, increases, and immortalizes your provision?

Result of Seed Consumed VS Result of Seed Separated and Sown

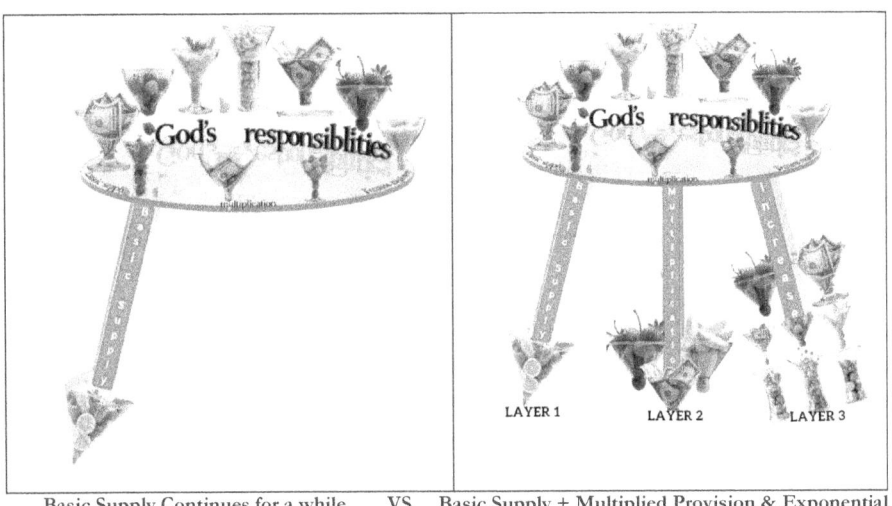

Basic Supply Continues for a while   VS   Basic Supply + Multiplied Provision & Exponential Supplies

Man's Responsibilities across the 3 Legs

As God carries divine responsibilities across the three sacred layers of provision, man too is summoned into partnership; expected to shoulder certain roles at each layer. Your seed is not just a provision; it is a prophetic vessel, steering you on this voyage to the destination of your choice, either toward the bountiful shores of prosperity or toward the barren wilderness of poverty. What you do, or fail to do, with your seed, determines which port you arrive at.

To neglect your responsibility is to reject the sacred laws that govern increase. It is to turn your back on the principles God Himself authored. And the moment you abandon your duty, you unconsciously release your seed into the stream that flows toward lack, insufficiency, and regret. There is no magic wand. There is no shortcut, no fervent prayer, no intense confession, no holy proclamation, that can redeem the seed that was never sown. The road to rags is well-travelled by those who prayed loud but acted small, who shout "abundance" but slept on principle.

At Layer One, the demand is clear: manage your basic supplies with intentionality. Discern the seed from the bread. Guard it. Sow it. For

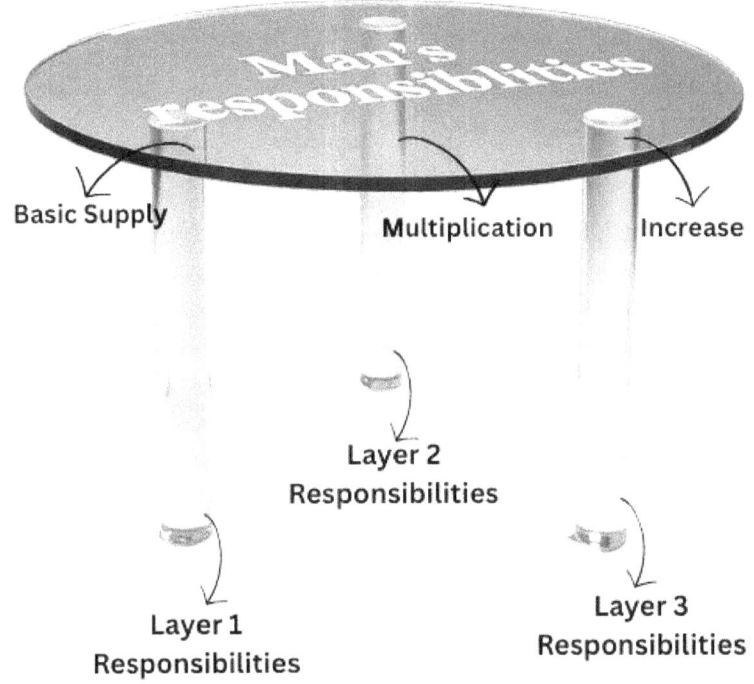

Man's responsibilities

here lies the foundation of your financial destiny. At Layer Two, where sown seed comes alive and returns in multiplied measures, the task escalates: you must now harvest, separate once again, and reinvest with strategy and discernment. Bread and seed arrive in greater measure, and so must your stewardship. This is the season to recruit skilled hands, to strengthen your barns, and fortify your vineyards.

But Layer Three, oh, Layer Three, is no place for the slothful or the complacent. It is a realm of exponential return, of overflowing vats and bursting storehouses, where fruits increase across multiple fields in quantum clusters. Yet with this divine deluge comes multiplied responsibilities greater than the former layers combined. You are now the keeper of streams and nations, and your wisdom, or lack thereof, can determine whether your fields blossom or break.

Man's Responsibility at Layer 1

Layer 1 Responsibilities

Watch Vineyard
Oversee and manage investments for optimal growth.

Sow Seed
Invest resources at the right time.

Prepare Field
Plan and prepare for future ventures.

Research Fields
Conduct thorough research before investing.

Increase Capacity
Enhance skills and knowledge for higher earning potential.

Keep Seed
Preserve future resources for future growth.

Eat Bread
Utilize current resources for immediate needs.

Separate Seed
Distinguish between current resources and future potential.

At the layer of basic supplies, it is your responsibility to:

1. Separate seed from bread;
2. Eat your bread;
3. Keep your seed properly—strictly for sowing;
4. Increase your personal capacity to earn more;
5. Thoroughly research a field, venture, or investment before sowing your seed;
6. Prepare your field or plan your venture and investment (with proper registrations and certifications);
7. Sow your seed into a well-known field (or second stream of income) and at the right time
8. Watch over your vineyard, venture, or investment; or hire someone to be in its charge.

Man's Responsibility at Layer 2

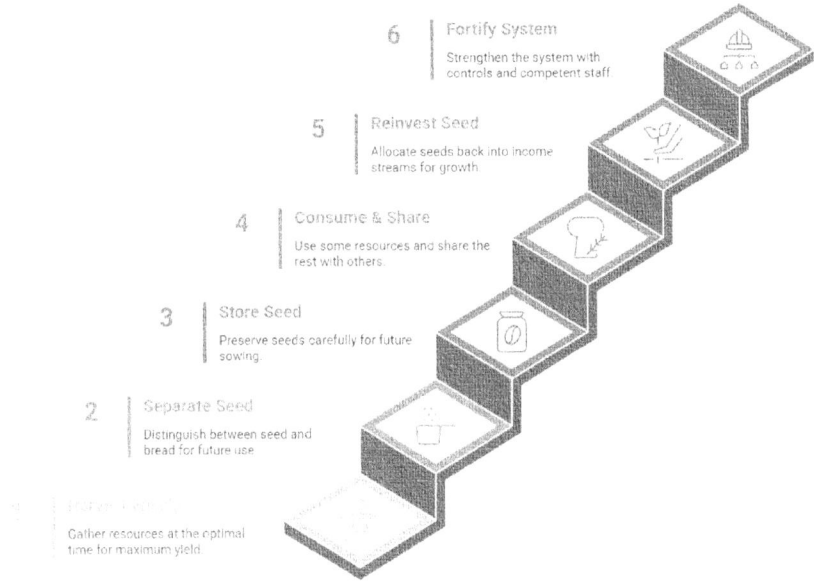

At the layer of multiplication, it is your responsibility to:

1. Harvest your field, venture, or investment at the right time;
2. Separate the seed portion from the bread portion of your harvest;
3. Keep your seed properly–precisely for enlarged sowing,
4. Eat some bread, share some bread and store the remaining for future use;
5. Push back your seed into your second income stream, field, venture, or investment; or consider a thirst income stream.
6. Fortify your field, venture, or investment with proper system and control
7. Hire competent hands to man the tiller.

Man's Responsibility at Layer 3

Layer 3 Responsibilities: Growth and Expansion

Layer 3 Responsibilities

- **Harvesting**
  - Multiple Fields
  - Ventures
  - Investments

- **Separation**
  - Seed Portion
  - Bread Portion
  - Fruit Portion

- Eat More Bread
- Share More Bread
- Store for Future Use

- **Value Creation**
  - Add Value
  - Dispense Fruits

- **More Hiring**
  - Competent Hands
  - Man the Tiller

- **Replanting**
  - New Territories
  - Existing Fields

- **Expansion**
  - Enlarge Field
  - Lengthen Cords
  - Strengthen Stakes

- **Fortification**
  - Proper Systems
  - Controls

- Grow Network
- Mentor Others

At the layer of exponential increase, it is your responsibility to:

1. Harvest your multiple fields, ventures, or investments.
2. Separate the seed portion from the bread and the fruit portions of your multiple harvests.
3. Eat more bread, share much more bread and store the remaining for future use.
4. Push back your multiple seeds into your multiple fields, ventures, and investments, and into new territories.
5. Create value with or add value to your fruits before dispensing.
6. Hire more competent hands to man the tillers
7. Enlarge the place of your field, lengthen its cords and strengthen its stakes.
8. Expand into multiple fields with the same seed or different seed breeds.
9. Fortify your multiple fields, ventures, or investments with proper systems and controls
10. Grow your network, and mentor others to continue wherever you hang the boot.

Your Seed is Your Key

This right here is one of the weightiest pivots of your stewardship, the moment you receive provision from the Lord's open hand. Whether it enters as hourly wages, daily profits, weekly returns, or monthly salaries… whether it flows in as allowances, commissions, bonuses, or comes in waves as royalties, deals, grants, inheritances, or dividends, what you've received is a sacred parcel. It is heaven's coded supply, neatly bundled with seed and bread. And if you look closely, with spiritual sight, you'll find the whisper of fruit waiting to break forth at the third layer, if only the journey continues. But hear this: the responsibility of what becomes of that bundle lies not with heaven anymore. It lies squarely on your shoulders.

Look at this verse of the scripture as a way of emphasising this principle one more time:

> **In the house of the wise are stores of choice food and oil, but a foolish man devours all he has**. Proverbs 21:20 (NIV)

Let me try to paraphrase the verse:

> Wise people save the choicest things because they don't spend all they make. On the other hand, fools spend all they get (or maybe even more).

Your most urgent duty is simple, but divine: **Spend less than 100% of your income**. Let me say that again, like a trumpet in your ears: **You must not consume it all**. You must discern the seed from the bread; and reserve the seed. That's your first step onto the hallowed path of surplus. That's how your voyage to abundance begins. With each seed kept, each portion spared, you carve out space for growth. You give room for multiplication. You permit increase.

But if you, like some described in the above verse, like many wise-in-their-eyes professionals, executives, and entrepreneurs, devour every dime, living as though seed were fiction, and bread were never-ending, you authorize your own limitation. You blockade the gates of layers 2 and 3 with your very own hands. Your finances may wear the fragrance of success, but they will crack under the pressure of time. Your progress will be chained to the basics. Not because God is unwilling, but because the principle has been violated. Fasting cannot undo it. Loud prayers may only echo louder warnings. The best they'll do is awaken your spiritual senses to this irrevocable truth.

Yet, for those who embrace this path, who shoulder their portion in this divine covenant, basic supplies shall not fail, multiplied returns shall not cease, and exponential increase shall rise like morning on the horizon. This is not a motivational line. It's heaven's strategy to usher you into the full flood of kingdom wealth and generational impact. Welcome to the principle that makes princes out of paupers.

Chapter 8

Seed-Bread Ratio

What proportion of your supply should you truly set apart as seed? Pause, reflect, and answer honestly. This isn't a law etched in stone, yet the principle is timeless. Some sow five percent, some ten, others twenty or fifty. There are those who set apart an entire month, or two, of their annual earnings. Many do it through modern systems, like standing orders or thrift contributions. Interestingly, standing order helps some to obey the principle unconsciously, separating their seed without even knowing they're dancing to the rhythm of heaven's ancient wisdom. It works nonetheless; because seed separation is a universal covenant, woven into the framework of increase. Whatever method you adopt, the truth stands inviolable: your journey to superabundance begins the moment you stop consuming all and start separating the seed, not for celebration, but for

Seed/Bread Ratio

cultivation; not for anniversary party cakes, but for investment in income-generating ventures.

Financial books and budget coaches may introduce you to models: 10%, 20%, even 25%. You may have heard of the famed 50/30/20 rule: 50% for essentials, 30% for wants, 20% for savings. And yes, these templates have their usefulness. But life is not one-size-fits-all. A single mother earning minimum wage cannot save the same percentage as a tech executive with a six-figure salary. A retiree living on pension cannot be expected to match the seed sowing of an entrepreneur in full swing.

Wisdom is knowing what to do, where you are, with what you have. Your age, your income tier, your debt profile, your responsibilities, your financial goals, these are the compass points that guide your seed proportion. If you're a high earner, it's wise to send more seed ahead. But if you're struggling to breathe under the weight of bills and loans, don't despise the day of small beginnings. Saving a little is better than consuming everything. Prioritize paying your debt.

This is the second step in the journey to enduring wealth: recognizing that every seed you don't separate is a harvest you'll never see. It's not about perfection; it's about progression. Start somewhere. Let your seed match your stage, but be sure it exists. And as your life improves, when debts are paid, bonuses flow, or opportunities blossom, let your seed grow too. Don't expand your appetite while shrinking your future. Learn the discipline of delaying your discretionary consumption so you can walk the discipline of accelerating your multiplication.

But remember: not all savings are seed. Your emergency fund is not your seed. The money you've tucked away for next term's fees, a car repair, or a short vacation, that's not seed. Seed is the portion that is not for eating today, nor spending tomorrow. It is the part of your provision with a future assignment. It is sacred capital, meant to be planted and watered, and watched until it becomes a tree, then a forest, and then a field yielding after its kind.

Now, while you discern your own path, let me offer you a compass: a biblical formula for such a time as this. I call it "Joseph's Formula." Stay with me. Let's uncover what heaven whispered to a slave-turned-statesman, whose wisdom fed nations and preserved generations.

The Joseph Formula for Seed: Bread Proportion

The Joseph Formula wasn't crafted in a boardroom or pulled from modern finance books, it was etched into Scripture from the very dawn of divine dealings with men. It first emerged in the book of Genesis, tucked within Pharaoh's palace, yet thundered from heaven's treasury. And though generations have passed, it remains there still, unchanged, unchallenged, and undefeated, awaiting any wise soul who dares to see, believe, and apply its timeless wisdom.

> **Let Pharaoh do this, and let him appoint overseers over the land, and take up a fifth part of the land of Egypt in the seven plenteous years.** Gen 41.34 (KJV)

> **And it shall come to pass in the harvest, that ye shall give a fifth part unto Pharaoh, and four parts shall be your own for seed of the field and for your food, and for those of your households and for food for your little ones.** Gen 47.24 (KJV)

Here, in the days of scarcity and surplus, Joseph unveiled a five-part system of stewardship, a sacred architecture for managing provision. He apportioned the income into five sacred channels: the king's portion, the seed portion, the food portion, the household's portion, and the youngsters' portion.

With divine precision, Joseph assigned twenty percent to Pharaoh, the governing system, and left the remaining eighty percent to serve the vital pillars of survival, continuity, and legacy. Following his trail, I choose to honour that wisdom by allocating equal weight to the four non-royal portions, recognizing each as non-negotiable in the voyage toward kingdom stewardship and generational abundance. Take a look at the depiction of the categories Joseph proposed and how I have allocated them into segments below:

Joseph's Formula for Seed/Bread Allocation

I have no shred of doubt about the integrity of this ancient formula, time has tested it, crisis has confirmed it, and outcomes have crowned it. Whether applied by a single soul or a sovereign state, it works, in times of plenty, and in seasons of famine. This divine blueprint was activated in a season of economic boom and sustained a nation through a grinding recession that spanned nearly a decade, with no bailout from heaven, just obedience to a heaven-inspired formula.

The brilliance of Joseph's framework is that it transcends scale. It applies to individuals, to families, to corporations, to communities, and even to governments.

However, because government systems in several nations deduct taxes at the source, your role begins from what remains: your profit, your take-home pay, your declared net earnings. That is where the stewardship begins. From that point forward, you are the governor of what flows in and what must flow out, guided by a formula that turns provision into preservation, and preservation into prosperity. That is what I will apply the formula to.

The formula presents us with these broad categories:

A. Bread
    a. For your food: consumption, emergency, & contingency.
    b. For your children: care, education, preservation.
    c. For your larger household: extended responsibilities, dependents, communities etc.

B. The King's portion: Spiritual investment, civic & societal obligations.

C. Seed for your field: production, reinvestment, skills-building.

The bread of your provision is designed to meet the daily realities of yourself, your children, and your community. It is meant for essentials and consumables. Herein lays your food and rent, your gas and subscriptions, your clothing and essentials. It includes care and education, extended responsibilities to dependents and your community, as well as today's emergencies and tomorrow's contingencies. A part of your bread may be consumed swiftly; some of it may be tucked into short-term savings for needs that lurk just around the corner; some may be used for a contingency buffer like insurance. This portion oils the wheels of life, but it does not drive you to destiny.

The second portion is the King's share: set aside for the altar, for the covenant, for divine alignment. This covers your tithe and offerings, your contribution to church projects, your donation to just causes in the society, for the welfare of your community, and for the poor. It is your honour to God, and your stake in the eternal economy.

But there is a third portion, equally sacred and often ignored, the seed meant for your own field. This is not tithes. This is not charity. This is not a tax. This is your economic destiny in raw form, entrusted to your stewardship.

As you set aside the King's portion and do not default on your taxes, don't forget your own field. This is because, while God promises to rain upon your land, and the government builds roads and policies to foster ease, it is still your responsibility to plant into your own soil. The heavens may release dew and the nation may create enabling structures, but without seed in your own field, nothing grows, nothing multiplies, and nothing increases. If you pay your taxes without owning an income-generating investment, you're not maximizing all the benefits of government policies. If you take part in Christian giving without seed sown in your own field, you limit your provision to the basic layer—even when your soil is fertile and heaven's shower falls on it.

Pay your tax if the law of your jurisdiction requires it. Honour kingdom responsibilities; it may be tithe covenant or something even deeper in scope, in requirements, and in consecration. There is no reason to measure everyone with a blanket gauge.

But even as you honour the altar and obey the state, do not neglect your seed. Your provision must not end at giving for godly causes or taxing for governance. It must find its way into your field, into ventures, enterprises, investments, systems, and soil, where it can be sown, nurtured, multiplied, and raised into clusters of enduring fruit. This is how your provision becomes prosperity. This is how your supply transcends survival and touches the realm of legacy.

Chapter 9

The King's Portion

The chain of poverty is rarely broken by mere effort or enthusiasm. It is often a deeply entrenched stronghold, fastened by generations of societal philosophies, hardened mindsets, cultural misdirection, and misinterpretations of heaven-backed financial principles. It binds not only wallets but worldviews. But like rusted iron dissolving beneath the steady drop of wisdom's rain, these age-old shackles can melt away when God's truth seeps into the soul of a man.

You see, beyond the daily grind of earning and spending lays a sacred garden, one pregnant with possibilities. It is here that dollars take root, ideas germinate, and obedience blossoms into sustainable wealth. These are not mere habits, but divinely aligned systems, hallowed patterns, that shape financial destinies. These habits are the stitches and strands that cultivate the rich soil of financial intelligence and nurture the seeds of your sweat into an experience of true abundance.

In this garden, the sweat of your brow is not wasted, it becomes water to your seed, and your seed becomes tomorrow's towering forest. All it takes is the courage to awaken to new patterns of thought and action, to plant with precision in the soil of understanding and tend your field with the wisdom of heaven.

If you've spent enough time in and around church circles, then you've surely encountered teachings on giving, tithes, offerings, firstfruits, and various calls to generosity. But amid these voices, half-truths often echo louder than wisdom, and many have stumbled through years of confusion, disillusionment, and even manipulation.

There are so many half-truths and misleading teachings about giving and sowing. There is, sadly, a glaring mix-up in understanding the difference between the King's portion and the seed for your own field. While your generosity toward God's house must be a sacred expression of reverence and love, never of compulsion, it is not to be mistaken for the strategic sowing of your seed into the ventures God has placed in your hands. One honours the throne; the other multiplies your yield. They are not interchangeable. One is vertical; the other is vocational. To confuse the two is to short-circuit the cycle of divine provision.

Joseph's formula, carved in scripture long before finance became a science, offers a roadmap for every faithful steward, one-fifth for the King, and four parts spread wisely across life's mandates. It's simple. It's spiritual. It's scriptural. And it works. Not as a legalistic noose, but as a liberating guideline. It ensures that honour is given to the King's field and investment is made into your own.

While you should honour the King's portion as it applies within the boundaries of your faith and personal consecration, you must guard against any delusion that doing so covers for the need to plant seeds in your field. Conversely, building your investment portfolio or growing your businesses is not a reason to neglect the King's portion or the King's field.

Yet, how curious it is that when God's provision seems modest, many claim it's not enough to separate anything for the King. And when He gives much, people then carry the calculator, and suddenly, 10% feels too large to honour the very Source of the surplus. So they split the tithe, pouring it into a cocktail of offerings, alms, and projects, as though God cannot discern proportions or do basic math.

A faithful steward does not slice the tithe into bits to appease conscience or crowd. Your tithe is your tithe. Render it as such. Your offerings are your offerings. Extend them beyond convenience. Your almsgiving, church projects, and mission contributions are sacred extras, not clever substitutes. If you embrace Joseph's formula in its wisdom and simplicity, you will find balance, not bondage, and you'll be spared from pulpit pressure and personal guilt alike. By that formula, pay your tithe and keep others like offerings and donations within another 10%. No amount of pulpit-pressing should move a mature Christian who fulfils the mandates of that scriptural formula unless there is a persuasion within his/her spirit.

I'm not imposing a rigid rulebook here. But I dare to recommend this framework, not from tradition, but from tested truth. A Christian steward is not being smart, splitting tithe into parts and spreading them over different courses. While you must walk according to your personal consecration, make sure it is a consecration that is consistent with the full counsel of Scripture, not one that cherry-picks generosity, massages disobedience, and selectively conforms to biblical directives. God doesn't need your split-tithe strategies; He desires your sincere stewardship.

God has a Field

If you sit with memory long enough, it won't be too long before you stumble upon a moment, maybe distant, maybe forgotten, when help came to you through hands you never knew, made possible by someone else's generosity. Whether it was a scholarship you received, a meal you didn't pay for, a church program that blessed you, a youth camp that lit a fire in your spirit, or a television or online broadcast that stirred you back to life, it was likely funded by unseen givers who sowed into the King's field.

And if you, as a believer, claim never to have benefited anything, directly or indirectly, through church-supported channels, perhaps you've at least heard of outreaches that fed the hungry, clinics that cared for the sick, or evangelistic crusades that led the lost into the saving arms of Jesus. These weren't orchestrated by angels dropping coins from heaven, but by faithful givers whose obedience and compassion made such movements possible. The King's field requires resources, real, tangible resource to run the errands of mercy and spread the fragrance of the gospel. To withhold your part is to withhold your hand from a field you've partaken of or may someday need.

So when the Spirit prompts you to give, whether a tithe, an offering, or a special gift toward mission and mercy, understand: you're not just funding a ministry. You're taking part in a divine cycle of giving and receiving, of pouring into lives you may never meet, yet whose stories will carry the fingerprint of your obedience.

Take a moment to glance through the next two pages, where I've highlighted just a handful, yes, only a glimpse, of the countless necessities and life-shaping programs that reflect the power and purpose of giving to the King's field. These few examples showcase the many ways your seed contributes to both local upliftment and global transformation, building communities, changing lives, and advancing the Kingdom of God across borders and generations

Name	Focus/Programs and Benefits	Impact and Reach
World Vision International	• Global child sponsorship, disaster relief, and community development • Comprehensive support to children in 100+ countries	• In 100+ countries • Approximately 3.5 million children worldwide
Samaritan's Purse, World Medical Mission	• Medical mission trips, free clinics, and evangelism worldwide • Emergency medical response in war-torn/disaster-affected areas. • Life-saving surgeries and treatments in underserved regions • Operation Christmas Child program – delivery of gift-filled shoeboxes to children. • Financial and legal support for persecuted Christians. • Water and sanitation projects	• Preventable deaths in war zones and impoverished areas • Critical, humanitarian aid in natural disaster zones • Medical care in conflict zones
Catholic Charities	• Comprehensive social services for the poor and immigrants. • Housing assistance and shelters for the homeless. • Food pantries and soup kitchens for those in need. • Counseling and job training programs for struggling individuals. • Critical support for disaster victims and vulnerable populations • Disaster relief and refugee resettlement	• Serves over 15 million people annually in United States and International,, regardless of religious affiliation
RCCG Charity Programs	• Hospitals, medical equipment supplies, free medical care for underprivileged communities. • Free schools and scholarship programs for children in need. • Food and housing aids for widows and orphans.	• Nigeria & International

The Salvation Army	• Emergency food aids & hunger relief programs to low-income families, homeless individuals, and disaster victims • Humanitarian aid, rehabilitation, and social services. • Homeless shelters and addiction recovery centers. • Emergency food aids and grocery packages • Job training and emergency disaster relief. • Youth mentorship and community development programs.	• Global, feeding millions annually
Hillsong CityCare	• Housing and counseling assistance for domestic violence survivors with. • Meals and financial support for struggling families. • Education programs and vocational training for disadvantaged youth. • Support to vulnerable individuals and families	• Australia & International
Christ Embassy's InnerCity Mission	• Food, clothing, and education to orphans, street children, and underprivileged youth. • Free medical outreach and health services for the poor. • Vocational training and empowerment programs for youth.	• Nigeria & International
International Justice Mission	• Anti-trafficking, modern slavery and violent oppression • Rescue operations for trafficking victims • Legal support for vulnerable populations • Community protection initiatives • Rehabilitation programs	• Works in 8 countries to protect the most vulnerable from violence
Living Water	• Clean and sustainable water solutions in developing regions • Drilling of wells, water treatment systems	• Has helped over 10 million people gain access to clean water

Organization	Activities	Impact
International	• Community hygiene and water management training	
Union Gospel Mission	• Temporary shelter, • Addiction recovery programs, • Job training, • Long-term housing solutions.	• Helps thousands escape homelessness and rebuild their lives in USA and Canada
Compassion International	• Orphan Care & Foster Support • Individual child sponsorship • Educational support • Healthcare and Nutrition programs • Vocational training • Christian discipleship	• Operates in 25 countries with a child-centered approach • Breaks cycles of poverty by empowering orphans and at-risk youth
Living Water International	• Clean Water Initiatives: drills wells, installs water filters, and teaches sanitation in villages without clean water	• Prevents waterborne diseases and reduces child mortality in Africa/Latin America countries
Prison Fellowship	• Prison Ministries & Reentry Programs • Provides Bibles, bible studies, vocational training, and post-release support for inmates.	• Lowers recidivism rates and restores families globally
African Christian Schools	• Educational Scholarships & Schools • Funds tuition, builds schools, and trains teachers in rural areas.	• Increases literacy and empowers future leaders in Africa
Youth With A Mission (YWAM)	• Comprehensive global missionary outreach and training • Discipleship training schools • Short-term and long-term mission trips • Community development projects • Multicultural evangelism	• Combines spiritual outreach with practical community support • Operates in over 180 countries

Organization	Activities	Focus
Campus Crusade for Christ	<ul><li>Evangelistic and discipleship outreach to university students and Young Adult</li><li>Provides Christian mentorship for college students.</li><li>Trains student leaders to share the Gospel on campuses.</li><li>Distributes Christian literature and digital evangelism resources</li></ul>	<ul><li>Reaches students in over 190 countries, focusing on spiritual mentorship and personal faith development</li></ul>
Operation Mobilization (OM)	<ul><li>Global Evangelism and Community Engagement</li><li>Missionary team deployments</li><li>Literature and media ministry</li><li>Cross-cultural evangelism training</li><li>Mission to challenging and restricted access region</li><li>Humanitarian aid and discipleship programs</li><li>Supports underground churches in persecuted nations</li></ul>	<ul><li>Mobilizes Christian missionaries to evangelize and disciple people in difficult-to-reach regions</li></ul>
Gideons International	<ul><li>Free Bible distribution and evangelism in hotels, hospitals, prisons, and schools</li><li>Place Bibles in hotels, schools, and public spaces</li><li>Support prison ministries with free materials.</li><li>Bible distribution in military bases</li><li>Personal evangelism and Bible study programs</li></ul>	<ul><li>Operates globally, making biblical texts accessible</li></ul>
Christ for All Nations (CfaN)	<ul><li>Large-scale Gospel campaigns and training of local evangelists & pastors</li><li>Hosts large-scale Gospel campaigns, sometimes attracting millions.</li><li>Trains local evangelists and pastors in church leadership.</li><li>Provides free Christian resources to new converts</li></ul>	<ul><li>Conducts mass evangelistic crusades, especially in Africa</li></ul>

Though a drop in the vast ocean that is the King's field, the programs outlined above offer a glimpse into the profound, transformative possibilities of church-supported ministries. These are not just charitable projects; they are living rivers of hope flowing into dry lands. Each one carries the scent of eternal impact, feeding the hungry, healing the sick, clothing the poor, and planting the Gospel where despair once reigned.

Now, pause and ponder: Which of the areas of focus, programs and benefits, impact and reach would you deem unnecessary? Which of them do you already support, if only once or twice a year, with a portion of your income? Are you waiting to become a multi-millionaire before parting with a fragment of your resources for the sake of the Kingdom?

If you truly mean business with your Christian stewardship, then let this truth settle deeply; a sacred portion of your earnings must be intentionally and consistently directed toward godly causes. Not out of compulsion, but out of conviction. Not to tick a religious box, but to fuel divine mandates across time and territories. And that can happen through any number of faithful platforms, local churches, global missions, kingdom outreaches, or discreet acts of compassion. What matters most is that your hands remain open, and your heart aligns with heaven's heartbeat.

The King's portion is connected to the following verses of the Bible:

- Your tithe – as applicable:

- - Bring ye all the tithes into the storehouse… Mal 3:10 (KJV)
- Your freewill offering or any kind of wilful sacrifice:
  - … bring all that I command you; your burnt offerings, and your sacrifices,…Deut 12:11 (KJV)
- Your giving to the poor (or charity):
  - Giving help to the poor is like loaning money to the Lord… Prov 19:17 (ERV)
  - And many such

Whatever name it bears in your own context, be it tithe, offering, sacrificial seed, almsgiving, or donation to noble causes, it all flows into one broad stream: the King's portion. Whether it's labelled a benevolence fund, a kingdom project, a mission's envelope, or a church building pledge, the essence remains the same, it is the portion set aside in honour of the King.

Not every believer is called or equipped to personally respond to disaster zones, establish food banks, or board a plane for cross-cultural missions. But through the platform of the Church, God's agency on earth, you can send your seeds where your feet may never go. You can share in the burden, bless the wounded, and be part of the kingdom's movement that stretches beyond borders and boundaries. For in the economy of heaven, the one who sends shares in the reward of the one who went. And by your giving, you take your place, not on the sidelines, but right in the heart of God's advancing purpose on earth.

Christian Giving

Christian giving is not a side ritual of faith; it is a sacred pulse in the heartbeat of discipleship. Rooted deeply in the soil of divine generosity, it echoes the Father's greatest gift, His only Son, given not as a loan but as a Lamb (John 3:16). It is not merely the motion of financial transaction, but the posture of a yielded heart; a spiritual discipline that pours out gratitude, worship, and obedience.

Yet, in this sacred space, chaos has sometimes crept in. What should be the fragrant offering of love has, in some circles, been stained with manipulation, commercialism, and gross misappropriation. There are leaders who ceaselessly manipulate and coerce the givers. There are even church leaders who divert and misuse moneys so sacrificially donated by the brethren. Congregants who once gave with joy now sit in silent resistance, hurt by mismanaged trust. Some leaders even parade their wealth like trophies in a contest for carnal validation, as though the altar were some runway.

Still, amidst these fractures, God has not abandoned His field. There remains a remnant, churches, ministries, and men, whose sole ambition is to stretch the frontier of the gospel with integrity, accountability, and holy fire. They weep over the lost, feed the poor without social media fanfare, raise missions that shine light into unreached corners of the earth, and steward every coin as a sacred trust.

Let me offer you this counsel: do not draw maps for your destiny using the compass of disillusioned critics. Don't let the noise of those stuck in cycles of unbelief become your soundtrack for stewardship. If your current church leadership lacks integrity, misplaces priorities, or trades kingdom vision for personal comfort, don't bury your seed in bitterness, but find where it can bloom. If your faith community's management is the kind that shows indifference to responsibility, suppresses the passion for mission, evangelism, and benevolence, and insatiably stimulates individual appetites for selfish gains, find a ministry where values and integrity have not eroded.

The King's field is wider than one man's personal cocoon or one organisation's programmatic appetite. Locate ministries where the soil is fertile, where the leaders' hands are clean and their hearts are aflame. Give where your sacrifice can become a seed, not where it feeds the self-indulgent ego of some self-seeking men or the excesses of some empire builders. In doing so, you honour the King, and you ensure your portion is planted not in shallow pots, but in the boundless fields of eternal impact.

The Need for Christian Giving

From Genesis to the Gospels, from the Law to the Letters, Scripture never trivializes giving, it exalts it as sacred worship, faithful obedience, and the tangible expression of love. When Abraham, fresh from battle, acknowledged Melchizedek's priestly authority and offered a tenth of his spoils, he wasn't just honouring a priest; he was honouring a principle. That principle would later be etched into the Mosaic Law, commanding the tithe to sustain the priesthood, maintain the sanctuary, and care for the poor, widow, orphan, and stranger. But when the curtain of the Old gave way to the covenant of the New, giving was not abandoned, it was elevated. Jesus did not command tithing by law, but He called His disciples to a higher generosity: one not driven by duty, but by love. The early Church didn't merely tithe; they shared all things in common, not under pressure, but out of a passion for the kingdom. Paul, writing by the Spirit, declared a truth that still echoes: "God loves a cheerful giver." And beyond that, the Spirit whispers still: "It is more blessed to give than to receive." In such giving lies the heart of the gospel, sacrificial, joyful, generous, and deeply divine.

Christian giving meets various needs, including:

1. Supporting the Work of the Church: Christian giving is not a casual gesture; it is the lifeblood that sustains the mission and machinery of the Church. From the pulpit to the pew, from the sanctuary to the streets, the gospel needs both feet and fuel to run its course. The maintenance of facilities, the labour of ministers, the logistics of outreach, the engine of mission, and the breath of compassion all demand financial supply. When the faithful give, the Church advances; but when they withhold, the mission stutters. The work of God must not be stalled for lack of provision.

2. Helping the Poor and Needy: At the heart of true religion beats a burden for the vulnerable. Scripture is unequivocal: caring for orphans, widows, and the weary is a divine obligation. Giving is our outstretched hand to those bent beneath the weight of life. It transforms pews into places of provision, and altars into avenues of compassion. As we give, we lend to the Lord Himself (Prov. 19:17), and He repays not just in kind, but in kingdom currency that outlasts time.
3. Funding Missionary Work and Kingdom Expansion: The gospel does not travel on wings; it journeys through messengers. Missionaries, church planters, Bible translators, outreach workers, these are the front-liners of the Kingdom, but their hands can only reach as far as the supply lines stretch. Crusades cost. Translations, printing, and distribution require expenses. Evangelism eats resources. Every soul won is often first a seed sown through someone's generosity. Your giving funds the footprints of the gospel across cities, continents, and cultures.
4. Community Development: The Church is more than a gathering of worshippers; it is a builder of futures. Through giving, schools are raised, hospitals erected, communities strengthened, and social programs birthed. Christian giving is a hammer in one hand and a lamp in the other: building lives and illuminating paths.
5. Emergency and Crisis Support: In a world shaking with wars, disasters, economic downturns, and personal crises, giving becomes a shelter in the storm. When floods rise and hope wanes,

the Church rises through the generosity of its people, providing shelter, food, medicine, and the ministry of presence. Your gift may not stop the storm, but it can certainly build an ark for someone else.

While some criticize institutional expenses in Christianity, these investments enable the very gatherings, evangelism, education, and community services that define church life.

Christian Stewardship Encourages the King's portion

You are a steward responsible to God, not someone who chooses to selectively obey His word when and where you choose. You are a steward, entrusted, not entitled. Your giving is not a performance, a plea for pity, or a stage for applause. You're certainly not giving as a mechanism to pity God and His course. It is not driven by guilt, ego, or a bid for pastoral approval. No, you give because you've been honoured with the sacred duty of advancing the King's field (the church). You give as a privilege to extend the frontiers of God's kingdom, as an act of your stewardship; not as an occasional fundraiser.

Christian giving is not a fundraiser's tool; it is a steward's trust. There are significant differences when you give as a steward than when you give as a fundraiser. The purposes are different; so are the relationships behind the giving, the goals, and the outcomes. When you give as a fundraiser, you respond to campaigns. But when you give as a steward, you respond to covenant. One seeks support for a project; the other offers obedience to a King. The relationship is deeper, the goal eternal, and the outcome transformative.

Some church leaders approach Christian giving like fundraising; making many believe that Christian stewardship is synonymous with fundraising. The two are quite different.

Here are a few differences that I have highlighted in the following table.

	Christian Stewardship	General Fund-Raising
Call to Give	Spirit-led	Greed/project/need/want-motivated
Purpose of Giving	Worship God	Fund a project, a course, or an activity
Goal of Giving	Serve God with accountability	Meet budget; pay the bills, earn some recognition
Realm of activity	Spiritual	Financial
Decision to Give	Transformational	Transactional, quid pro quo
Source of Resources	God	Donors, financiers
Guiding Principle	Bible	Social responsibility
Motivation to Give	Fulfill spiritual responsibility, vows or discipleship needs	Satisfy sentiments, personal or institutional needs,
Disposition to Giving	Willingness, liberality	Willingness, Show, Competition
Personal return on investment	Joy of giving, blessing of obedience to God	Self-satisfaction; tax incentives
Primary outcome of giving	Advance God's course, bonding with God	Accomplish a personal motive, advance a course
Reasons for not Giving	Ignorance of responsibility, lack of commitment to God, confusion about responsibility, weariness from leadership coercion	Skepticism, caution, prefer other opportunities, no room for showmanship

Christian Stewardship's Giving Index

a. **Giving must be a joyful expression, not a frowning obligation.** You've likely received something from someone whose face said, "I'd rather not." And you knew, they were forced, not willing. Now imagine how God feels when your hand stretches out in offering, but your heart stays clenched in reluctance. He doesn't delight in duty-givers, only in those whose generosity dances with joy.

b. **God is not asking you to give what you do not have.** He's not impressed by reckless gestures that leave your family hungry or homeless. Christian stewardship is not a race of comparison or a game of spiritual competition. Your giving is deeply personal, measured by your means, not anyone else's metrics. Since you're not giving for human applause, the only audience that matters is God. And He doesn't grade your sacrifice by someone else's scoreboard.

c. **There are moments, divinely rare moments, when God Himself stretches you** (2 Corinthians 8:3). Not the pulpit, not a fundraising gimmick, but the Spirit. You'll feel it: the inner nudge to give beyond your comfort (not above your means), an offering that requires faith on your part. These are not standard protocols. These are not the rule or the norm, and no one is expected to make a by-law out of such. They are Spirit-led exceptions. No formula, no pressure, just faith. But beware: any pulpit that turns such rare obedience into regular compulsion is waving a red flag.

d. **Never give under duress**. Never sow with a sour spirit. You're not trying to pacify an angry deity, nor are you pleasing a scorekeeping angel. You are a son, not a slave. You are a daughter, not a bondwoman. God's heart delights in cheerful givers, not in those dragged by guilt or performance. God wants your giving to be a joyous experience, not a toiling requirement. Let your giving be a "want to," never a "have to." If it isn't born from love and laced with joy, pause. Revisit your motive before your money moves.

e. **Joseph's straightforward formula is still gold**. It guards your generosity with structure, ensuring the King's portion doesn't rob your own field, or the mouths and needs of your household. It's not a law, but a light. It is an effective tool to use in determining whether you are giving below or above practical biblical thresholds. And if there's ever a divine detour, a moment the Spirit urges an extraordinary sacrifice, make that move with clarity and reverence based on the soothing duologue of the Holy Spirit with your human spirit, not because of pressure. But return to your rhythm once you play the part that the Spirit of God (again, not the pulpit) demands of you. In fact, if every member of the household of God simply honoured their part as suggested by Joseph's formula, the storehouse of God would overflow, without the need to pulpit-press and sermon-compel anyone to go beyond that call of duty.

f. **Before giving, seek the Holy Spirit's guidance.** Far too many church projects branded "God's Work" today are driven not by divine instruction, not by obvious need, but by ego, rivalry, and personal ambition cloaked in religious jargon. Some pastors launch building projects to outshine the grandeur of the church down the street. Some others create unnecessary ministries just to keep up appearances, fund-raise endlessly to pad status, popularity, or push media empires that serve more of vanity platforms than Kingdom advancement. The motives behind some mega auditoriums, schools, campgrounds, relocation to highbrow areas, lavish interior redesigns and expensive decor upgrades might be more self-serving than divine instruction or genuine kingdom impact. Some initiatives exist solely to impress denominational hierarchies or justify inflated titles. Believers must be discerning: not every project branded "for the Lord" is birthed by His Spirit. Before giving, every Christian must pause, pray, and seek the Holy Spirit's guidance; because when the veil is lifted, the true motive often isn't mission, but manipulation. Your giving is sacred. Don't fund what and where God hasn't sent you.

How is Christian Giving Utilised?

Ever wondered where your giving actually goes?

It's more than envelopes, tithing apps, or offering baskets. When you give, you're not just supporting a church; you're fuelling a movement that touches lives in visible and invisible ways.

Your giving is utilized in two broad ways:

A. Local Church Allocation (Your First Field)

Most local churches steward your generosity across five vital areas:

1. Personnel: - From the pastor who counsels late into the night to the administrator who keeps the engine running, salaries and stipends ensure leaders can serve without distraction.
2. Facilities: - Lights, heat, chairs, sound, the physical space that welcomes worshippers weekly is powered by your support
3. Programs: - Children's classes, marriage workshops, youth events, discipleship and Sunday school resources… it's all funded by people like you.
4. Missions: - That evangelistic outreach in the inner city? That church plant overseas? That printed Bible in a language someone just read for the first time? Those tracts, devotionals, and self-help guides? You had a hand in it.
5. Benevolence: - Quietly, compassionately, many churches step in when life breaks down: groceries for a widow, rent for a struggling

family, school fees for a child.

B. Para-church and Non-profit Distributions (Beyond the Building)

Christian giving doesn't stop at the steeple. It stretches into specialized ministries that focus on needs many churches can't tackle alone:

1. Humanitarian Relief: - You're feeding hungry kids, clothing street children, rescuing trafficking victims, aiding disaster zones, sponsoring medical missions, providing wheelchairs, funding food pantries and soup kitchens, and helping widows rebuild their lives.
2. Education: - You're keeping seminary lights on, sponsoring future Christian teachers, and sending young dreamers to school.
3. Media Ministry: - From late-night sermons on TV to Bible apps downloaded by the millions, your giving funds truth in the digital age
4. Advocacy: - You're backing voices that confront systemic injustice, advocate for the vulnerable, and stand up where others stay silent.
5. Specialized Outreach: - You're showing up behind prison walls, in rehab centres, on college campuses, and among unreached tribes.

Your giving is not a donation; it's a deployment. Every naira or pound, dollar or dime becomes seed sown into lives, futures, and eternity. So next time you give, don't just see the basket. See the people. See the fatherless. See the broad King's field.

You're not just supporting a church. You're lighting up the world.

Falsehood and Manipulative Coercion in Christian Giving

Christian giving, when corrupted, can drift far from truth, integrity, and ethical principles. It morphs into various forms of false teachings and manipulative tactics. What was meant to be a joyful act of worship becomes a guilt trip, a performance, or a profit scheme.

Below are some of the most common ways falsehood and coercion creep into Christian giving, twisting Scripture, exploiting emotion, and burdening believers with pressure God never intended.

1. *The Prosperity Gospel & Seed-Faith Giving (Turning Generosity into a Transaction):*

Perhaps the most damaging distortion of Christian giving is the Prosperity Gospel. It promises divine payouts for earthly deposits, suggesting that the more you give financially, the more God is obligated to bless you materially. This is the theology behind "seed-faith giving," where you're told to sow a financial seed (usually into a preacher's ministry) to unlock a miracle or a financial breakthrough. To the proponents of this doctrine, generous giving is projected to be all about giving large sums of money. This lopsided teaching manipulates believers into giving with the expectation of personal gain or "financial miracle", rather than an act of faith and out of love for God and others. It reduces giving to a transactional relationship and distorts the true nature of the gospel of Jesus Christ.

<u>The Claim</u>:

- Some preachers claim that sowing a financial seed into their ministry will always result in multiplied returns, often claiming God is obligated to multiply whatever is thus "sown".
    - "Plant this seed and watch your bank account multiply."
    - "Your miracle is waiting on your money."
    - "God must respond when you give sacrificially."

<u>The Reality</u>:

- While God honours generosity, He is not a transactional deity. Giving should not be viewed as a transaction where money gets exchanged for divine rewards. True giving flows from love, not leverage. Many faithful givers remain in financial struggles, while those who promote this teaching often become wealthy at their expense.

Wake-up Call: This false teaching often pressures struggling believers into giving beyond their means and seduces the hopeful into giving for selfish gain, not godly worship. It trades the gift of giving for the gamble of returns. But God's blessings are not always financial, and His promises are never for sale. Sowing works when you sow in your field of value exchange: in obedience, with understanding, and in line with divine timing. The blessing is in the principle, not the pressure.

2. *Fear-Based Giving (The Gospel of Guilt and Threats)*:

Some ministries use threats of curses or divine punishment to pressure members into giving. People are told that if they don't give, especially tithes, they'll fall under curses, experience financial ruin, or block their blessings. Verses are twisted, motives are hijacked, and spiritual coercion becomes the norm. Their tactics instil fear rather than encourage faith and cheerful giving, putting folks under duress.

The Claim:

- Some preach that those who do not pay tithe will suffer financial losses, sickness, or misfortune as divine punishment.
    - "If you don't tithe, you're robbing God, and He will repay."
    - "Your health and wealth depend on your giving."
- Some claim tithing (giving 10%) is a requirement for salvation, answered prayers, or protection from curses.
    - "No tithe, no protection."

The Reality:

- The New Testament encourages generous giving, but never as a requirement for salvation. Besides, believers do not suffer any misfortune if they don't succumb to such fear-full tactics. Jesus freed us from the curse of the law (Galatians 3:13), including financial manipulation masked as spiritual law. Our giving is meant to be cheerful, willing, and Spirit-led, not forced by fear.

Wake-up Call: Fear is not a fruit of the Spirit. Giving out of terror, guilt, or superstition is not biblical obedience, it's spiritual abuse. 2 Corinthians 9:7 makes it clear: "Each of you should give what you have decided in your heart to give… not reluctantly or under compulsion." If you're being forced to give to prove your faith, you're not hearing from God, 0079ou're being stage-managed by men. And manipulation, no matter how well-packaged, is not kingdom service.

3. High-Pressure and Public Shaming Tactics (Turning the Pulpit into a Manipulator's Stage):

You don't need false doctrine to be deceived, just the right mix of guilt, fear, and a microphone. Some churches don't ask. They corner. They don't appeal. They coerce. And under the bright lights of trust, vulnerability is exploited. Even without adopting outright false doctrine, some spiritual leaders, those meant to guide, nourish, and protect, sometimes become emotional extortionists, using psychological pressure, public shaming tactics, and full-volume sermons to shake your pocket instead of your soul. These tactics, which exploit trust and vulnerability, include:

Common Manipulation Tactics

Forced Pledges: Members asked to stand, raise hands, or declare specific amounts publicly, while cameras roll and ushers hover.

- Guilt-Soaked Sermons: Messages designed not to lift burdens, but to load them, with shame, performance, and self-doubt.
- Emotional Triggers: "Urgent needs," "emergencies," and "heaven-or-hell moments" theatrically staged to stir irrational giving.
- Widow's Last Dime Doctrine: Comparing you to the widow in Scripture and pressuring you to match her "sacrificial giving" by handing over your last dollar, rent, or school fees.
- Donor Hierarchies: Bigger givers get better seats, louder applause, and invisible halos. Small givers? Ignored or pitied.

Extreme cases:

- Demanding access to your bank account in the name of "financial accountability" or "discipleship."
- Publicly calling out non-givers to shame, suspend, or excommunicate them.

- Tying ministry benefits and participation to tithing compliance.
- Urging people to max out credit cards, take loans, or give their last dollar as "a step of faith." with the promise that God will "supernaturally provide."

<u>The Claim</u>:

- "If you truly love God, you will give sacrificially." "Those who don't give to certain projects or programs prove they don't trust Him."
- "God told me there are 5 people here with $5,000, don't delay your miracle."
- "Give $1,000 seed for that miracle you are expecting."
- "If you don't give $1,000 tonight, you're blocking your blessing!"
- "We're in a financial crisis: if you don't give now, the ministry will collapse."
- "Call this line now; our pastor is waiting to release your healing through your seed."

<u>The Reality</u>:

- These are not invitations to generosity, but ambushes of faith. They are not spirit-led. They are stage-managed. They are not biblical. They are manipulative theatre, complete with rehearsed testimonials and guilt trips. Biblical giving should never be forced or guilt-driven.

- Jesus commended the widow in Mark 12:41–44, not because someone pressured her to give her last coin, but because her giving was pure, willing, and born of love, not fear.
- While legitimate needs exist, lying for donations is fraud. Proverbs 12:22 says, "Lying lips are an abomination to the Lord." That includes manufacturing emergencies or prophesying price-tagged miracles.
- 1 Peter 5:2–3 warns leaders not to "lord it over" God's people, but when pastors shame, rank, and emotionally blackmail givers, they're not shepherds. They're spiritual tyrants in clerical robes.

Wake-up Call: These practices are not merely "unethical fundraising", they are spiritual abuse, which exploits growing and vulnerable believers, undermines the voluntary nature of biblical giving, and manipulates emotions rather than encourages genuine generosity. They've driven many into debt, trying to buy God's attention. They've driven others away from church altogether, burned, bruised, and bitter.

Let it be clear: God does not only bless those who give in hundreds or thousands. He is not deaf to the widow, the job-seeker, the single mother, or the faithful steward with little in hand. He does not whisper miracle amounts to guest ministers while ignoring the actual needs and capacities of His children.

It is very okay for church leaders to announce the need in the ministry and the amount of money required to meet it. However, any preacher: based anywhere or invited from anywhere, who declares that only those who give $1,000, $5,000, or "whatever God told me" will be healed, blessed, or married, is most likely listening to the god called Mammon in the Bible, or its kinsfolk, the flesh. This is because the God who gave His Son freely doesn't sell breakthroughs behind a paywall. He knows the various categories of people in the congregation. He does not distribute to those who can give $1000 and above and then withholds from those whose capacity is just a fraction of that amount. Don't be deceived. Those who insist that you must give up to a certain amount of money to receive God's intervention in your family, business, health, or any other area are often not being sincere with you.

4. Unverified Miracle Promises (the Marketplace of Manipulation): One of the most disturbing distortions of Christian giving today is the commercialization of the miraculous. Church altars have become marketplaces where oil is auctioned and hope is sold to the highest bidder. From "anointed" oils and waters to "holy" wristbands and soaps, the faithful are lured to buy their way into healing, favour, success, or breakthrough. Some church leaders who visited Israel even return with items mentioned in the Bible, like mustard seed, cinnamon, water from the River Jordan, and suck like, that they claim possess spiritual or miraculous powers to bring healings and financial prosperity. Such "anointed" items must be purchased or otherwise accessed with a minimum amount in offering or donation. Examples of such include:

1. "Anointed" Items

- Anointed oil–just regular olive or vegetable oil, often sold as a miracle-working substance.
- Anointed water–bottled or tap water, sometimes with food colouring, claimed to heal or bring favour.
- Anointed handkerchiefs–regular fabric pieces marketed as healing or deliverance tools.
- Anointed sand, stones, or salt–supposedly collected from "holy" grounds or some miracle mountains.

2. Miracle Consumables

- Special "holy" soap–promoted as a substance that washes away curses, attracts wealth or favour.
- Spiritual perfumes or sprays–said to bring love, success, or protection.
- Miracle seeds or fruits–sold with promises of financial breakthrough upon planting or eating.

- Prayer cakes, rice, or drinks–claimed to have been prayed over for specific breakthroughs.

3. Ritual Tools

- Prayer wristbands or necklaces–often plastic or cheap beads, said to protect or bring miracles.
- Customised spiritual calendars or posters–with dates marked as "miracle days" or for "prophetic insight".
- Holy mantles or garments–pieces of cloth or clothing sold as carrying divine presence.

4. Fake Spiritual Services

- Prophetic consultations– paid one-on-one sessions to receive prophecies or spiritual guidance.
- Deliverance sessions– often dramatized events requiring a fee or "seed sowing."
- Miracle prayer lines or call-ins– where people pay to receive blessings or prayers remotely.

5. Symbolic Acts

- "Sowing seeds" for miracles– coaxing people to give money or valuables for divine intervention.
- Selling testimonies– staged or false miracle stories used to induce more giving.

There are those who 'anoint' work tools like scissors, pens, car keys, uniforms, and such likes as you oblige them by parting with some money. Some promise prophetic utterances and varying degrees of prayers and fasting to those who meet payment thresholds. Some others assure specific miracles for money, as though God's blessings are for sale.

<u>The Claim</u>:

- "Buy this anointed item and receive healing."
- "Sow a seed to receive a miracle."
- "Pay for a deliverance session and your doors will open."
- "Bring a token and we'll fast and prophesy for your promotion."

The Reality:

- The grace of God is not for sale. Jesus never traded miracles for money. Acts 8:18–20 is still in your Bible, Simon the Sorcerer tried to purchase spiritual power, and Peter rebuked him sharply. God does not require you to pay for His attention, power, or blessing. He requires your faith, your obedience, and your walk.

Wake-up Call: If you are buying oils, mantles, holy soaps, or subscribing to miracle call-lines and prophetic consultations for a fee, you are not being blessed; you are being exploited. You are being manipulated with a counterfeit gospel that leverages your pain and desperation to feed a false spiritual economy. These tactics are spiritual scams wearing religious clothing. It is not faith, it is superstition, fear, and transactional religion. God is not a merchant. He is your Father. And His love cannot be bought. If you are falling for this tactic (wherever or by whomsoever), you are most likely being scammed!

5. *Exaggerated Testimonies and False Claims (Manufactured Miracles)*: Another deadly tactic in manipulative giving is the use of exaggerated or outright fabricated testimonies. They cook up stories of people who supposedly gave and instantly became millionaires, won contracts, built their own houses, gave birth to twins after waiting for years, and much more. These are emotional triggers and engineered stories designed to hook the hopeful and guilt the hesitant.

The Claim:

- "She gave her last $100 and became a millionaire in a week."
- "He sowed a seed and won a government contract the next day."
- "After giving all she had, she gave birth to twins after 10 years of barrenness."
- "A car accident was miraculously averted because of a tithe paid."

The Reality:

- Claims that tithing and giving turned people into millionaires, made them conceive, prevented job loss, accidents, or family crises are unproven.
- Many of these stories are unverifiable, over-dramatized, or outrightly staged. Giving can be a channel of blessing, but it does not override the principles of stewardship, process, obedience, and time. We're called to faith, not fantasy.

Wake-up Call: These miracle tales often overshadow the daily lives of sincere believers who've been faithful and are still waiting, waiting for healing, waiting for a child, waiting for a breakthrough. Instead, pulpit hawkers seize the occasion of their need and lack to exploit their faith. They stir unhealthy comparisons and plant seeds of discontent and self-doubt. "Why hasn't it worked for me?" becomes the silent question tormenting those who gave with honest hearts. Giving is not a spiritual vending machine. God is not coerced by pressure or manipulated by offerings. He is sovereign, and His timing is holy. If miracles must be exaggerated to encourage giving, then the altar is no longer holy: it's a stage. We do not need fireworks to validate God's power. His grace is often quiet, progressive, and deeply personal. Stop running after those using miracle marketing to prey on people's struggles.

6. *Misuse of Scripture to Justify Unwarranted* Giving (Weaponized Bible verses): Another dangerous deception is weaponized Bible verses. Passages like Matthew 19:21, where Jesus tells the rich young ruler to sell all he has and give to the poor, are wrenched out of context and wielded like swords against the spiritually hungry. Some pastors use these verses to demand everything in your bank account, wallet, or purse, as though reckless giving will unlock immediate miracles in 24 hours or 7 days.

The Claim:

- Give all your salary to receive a twenty-four hours miracle.
- "Empty your account and God will fill your life within seven days."

- "The more painful your sacrifice, the more powerful your reward."
- "God is waiting on your zero to give your overflow."

<u>The Reality</u>:

- Jesus, in Matthew 19:21, was not issuing a universal command for giving. He was exposing a personal idol. That moment was about surrender, not prescription. It was a heart diagnosis, not a church doctrine. God doesn't need your last dollar to prove Himself. He needs your obedience, not your desperation.

Wake-up Call: Yes, radical giving exists. But it must be Holy Spirit-led, not pulpit-forced. True giving begins with revelation, not emotional hype. It's not about dumping your rent in the offering plate because of an excited sermon, but about discerning what God is actually asking of you. When Scripture is weaponized, hearts are wounded and wallets are emptied. But when Scripture is rightly divided, hearts are healed and giving becomes worship again. The Bible is clear that "Each of you should give what you have decided in your heart to give, not reluctantly or under compulsion, for God loves a cheerful giver." (2 Corinthians 9:7). Please take a moment to read that in some simpler-to-understand translations:

"You must each decide in your heart how much to give. And don't give reluctantly or in response to pressure. For God loves a person who gives cheerfully. "(NLT)

"Each of you must make up your own mind about how much to give. But don't feel sorry that you must give and don't feel you are forced to give. God loves people who love to give. "(CEV)

"I want each of you to take plenty of time to think it over, and make up your own mind what you will give. That will protect you against sob stories and arm-twisting. God loves it when the giver delights in the giving. " (MSG)

What True Biblical Giving Looks Like

After all the noise, gimmicks, and manipulated hype, what does real Christian giving actually look like? What is the kind that pleases God, not man, the kind that multiplies meaning, not just money?

Here's the truth, clean, clear, and unbought:

1. **True Giving Starts from Revelation, Not Manipulation**. God is not moved by amounts. He's moved by alignment. When the Holy Spirit

stirs your heart to give, whether large or small, it flows from clarity, peace, and joy. Not pressure, not panic, not peer performance.

2. **True Giving Flows from Relationship, Not Religious Ritual**. It's not about ticking a box. It's about reflecting God's nature. Giving is one way we mirror our generous Father. It's not a bribe, barter, or "payment" for blessings; it's an act of worship.

3. **True Giving Is Rooted in Stewardship, Not Superstition**. Giving doesn't cancel irresponsibility. God honours those who give AND steward. A man who doesn't budget but keeps sowing into every flashy promise is not exercising faith; he's practicing financial foolishness.

4. **True Giving Doesn't Harm Your Family or Health**. God never commands you to give at the expense of your family's well-being. If your generosity leads to guilt, neglect, or unnecessary suffering at home, it's not Spirit-led, it's showmanship disguised as sacrifice.

5. **True Giving Trusts God's Timing, Not Timelines from the Pulpit**. Real giving does not demand 24-hour miracles, 7-day breakthroughs, or "this-month marriage testimonies." God is not your genie. He is your God. And He works in divine timing, not in emotional blackmail.

6. **True Giving Is Spirit-Led, Not Crowd-Driven**. Give what the Lord impresses on your heart, not what the preacher says others are giving.

You're not here to impress heaven's accountant; you're here to obey heaven's whisper.

7. **True Giving Keeps Heaven in Focus, Not Earthly Return.**
Sometimes, your giving won't come back as money. It might return as peace, favour, healing, or protection. Sometimes it won't return visibly in your life, but will multiply through others. And that's okay.

If your giving isn't bringing you closer to God, something is wrong.

If your giving is producing anxiety, not assurance, pause and pray again.

If your giving feels like spiritual blackmail, it probably is.

- Give as sons and daughters, not slaves.
- Give with joy, not guilt.
- Give in faith, not fear.

That's the giving heaven receives.

Diversions and Misappropriation of Church Funds

This is one of the hardest truths in the faith walk: while many Christian organizations handle money with transparency and honour; some have fallen into the pit of financial mismanagement and spiritual hypocrisy. The result? Scandals that shake believers, rattle seekers, and smear the gospel with a stain that takes decades to wash away.

Let's not mince words. Some church leaders do not just mishandle resources; they funnel them into personal kingdoms of luxury and self-glorification. Designer suits, fleets of luxury cars, private jets, mansions purchased off the backs of sacrificial givers: these stories aren't rare outliers anymore. They're headlines. They're wounds. They're poison in the well of trust.

Worse, many congregations are kept in the dark. No reports, no accountability, no transparency. People give with faith, expecting stewardship, only to see their resources become playthings for personal ambition. Meanwhile, members suffer. Bills pile up. Children go hungry. The church preaches faith but practices secrecy.

The book of Acts shows us a church where "there was not a needy person among them." Contrast that with today, where some pulpits drip with gold while the pews buckle under unpaid rents and hungry families. This is not merely unfortunate. It is anti-Christ.

Then there's the showmanship, the brazen, public flaunting of wealth. Some call it "evidence of divine blessing." But what gospel is this that builds marble towers while ignoring the crumbling homes of the widow, the orphan, the single mother who scrapes together her tithe with trembling hands? A gospel that trades character for cash is no gospel at all. Jesus flipped tables over this kind of spiritual market.

Believers' Posture to Giving

Yet let us not throw away the baby with the dirty bathwater. At its best, Christian giving is sacred. It is proof that our resources belong to God, that generosity is divine DNA, that money can become fuel for relief, hope, and transformation. When practiced with integrity, discernment, and genuine compassion, Christian giving becomes a powerful expression of faith, love, and obedience to God that transforms both giver and recipient, advances the gospel, and brings glory to God.

For believers navigating these waters, the journey involves both heart examination and practical wisdom, cultivating generous spirits while exercising responsible stewardship. I counsel you to take part in this fulfilling practice in ways that truly reflect the compassion, integrity, and transformative power at the heart of your faith. But, it is essential to practise your Christian giving with knowledge and practical discernment, like:

- Prayerfully seeking divine guidance about giving decisions.
- Giving according to your ability rather than someone else's hype.
- Examining each organizational focus and effectiveness before contributing.
- Supporting various causes (diverse portfolio) across local, national, and global needs.
- Periodically reviewing giving patterns and their alignment with your convictions and values.

The Christian tradition of giving affirms both sacrificial generosity and prudent stewardship. When properly practiced, it's a powerful tool for advancing God's kingdom by sharing your income beyond your immediate family, helping the needy, and fostering genuine faith among believers.

So give, but do it with eyes open, with heart clean, with spirit free from manipulation. Give because you believe in the mission, not because you were cornered by theatrics. Give because you serve a God who gave His Son freely, not because someone promised you a seat on the prosperity train.

And to church leaders: remember, this is God's money, not yours. He sees the ledger. He weighs the heart. And His patience with corruption is not endless.

The gospel is free. Steward the resources of God's people with fear, humility, and integrity; because giving isn't about big offerings on stage. It's about big hearts on a mission.

How Do Some Upright Church Leaders Acquire their Wealth?

How do some upright church leaders build true wealth? They walk the timeless road of divine principles laid bare in this very book. They take a portion of every provision God brings their way and sow it faithfully:

into the King's field and into their own. Their investments are not limited to sacred soil alone; they dare to build, to plant, to nurture fields of honest enterprise, inside and outside the church. They do not rob God to feed themselves, nor do they starve their own households in a frenzied piety that leaves their fields barren.

I'm therefore amazed when I see church members prayerfully expecting lasting riches while neglecting the principles that underscore the process. I just can't find in the Bible how people expect to attain financial riches by eating their seed or giving all in church and then praying, while neglecting the principles that their rich and upright leaders hold tenaciously to. That is not the way of the kingdom.

That's like expecting magic instead of miracles. You may find that elsewhere, but not in the true church.

When the Israelites received the miraculous supplies of manna in the wilderness, none of them became financially rich through that phenomenon. It was all consumed as they were instructed! But the indulgence of "consume it all" ended as soon as they ate something (fruit of harvest) whose yield encased seed and bread.

Then the manna ceased!

The manna ceased even though both provisions came from God. The manna ceased even though it was quicker and less laborious to gather.

There would have been a recession after just a year if they had failed to sow from that moment onward. If you want to truly experience lasting financial riches in this kingdom, you cannot continue to consume all of your supplies as manna, even if you are a pastor. Doing so will keep you perpetually in need. Manna-like consumption does not make anyone rich. It comes overnight and goes overnight. God does not intend that your manna-like supplies will be forever. You must recognize the difference between the season of manna and the season of seed and bread; and then act according to the principles of your season.

Daily bread may rain overnight. But riches do not rain instantaneously in God's kingdom. They grow through the steady hands of those who discern their season and act with patience, faith, and holy wisdom.

Consume all your provisions like manna, and you may be full for a fleeting night, but the dawn will reveal your emptiness again. It goes as quickly as it comes, sometimes before it even comes. Then you will come into chronic need again, in a day or two, or in a year or two. But if you honour the laws of seed and bread, separating, sowing, nurturing, waiting, it is only a matter of time before your planted seed becomes a forest of fruit-bearing trees, with branches that outlive you and roots that feed generations.

Below are some of the legitimate ways in which rich, upright pastors build their wealth.

A. **Primary Methods** (the flow begins here): These are basic income generation strategies.
1. Salary and benefits from their labour in the King's field.
2. Christian giving: gifts and offerings sent from grateful hearts into their ministry
3. Honorariums from speaking engagements.
4. Conference hosting, where wisdom meets eager listeners
5. Partnership programs, often birthed from trust with faithful followers.
B. **Secondary Methods**: Here, the wise steward reinvests. Seeds from the primary channels are sown into personal growth and multiple revenue streams:

Results:

1. More speaking engagements and paid appearances at conferences and events.
2. Sales of books, devotionals, and DVDs refined through deeper personal development and discipline.
3. Devotionals built through personal quiet time (and personal development).
4. Media productions: podcasts, TV shows, flowing from their personal study and intimacy with God.
5. Online courses and digital contents expanding their reach

6. Building a personal brand that stretches beyond the walls of a local assembly
7. Growing social media platforms and global audiences
8. Monetizing YouTube channels, podcasts, and blogs
9. Investments in stocks, cryptocurrency, or hedge funds.

C. **Tertiary Method**: Then comes diversification.
- Seeds from secondary income levels are further reinvested in personal development (which, in turn, brings them into higher levels of authority in their domain),
- Additional seeds become diversified into businesses (which leverage exposures, networks and partnership potentials in and outside the church), and
- Personal brand and wider audience lead to strategic networking with donors, corporate sponsors and international ministry connections.

Results:

1. Book deals, royalties from bestsellers that carry their voice far beyond the pulpit (this is much bigger than personal sales since great and bestselling Christian books generate massive royalties).
2. Media empires: Christian TV networks, streaming services, faith-based films, and documentaries. Christian TV Networks & Streaming Services (e.g. TBN, Daystar, LoveWorld TV, The

Potter's Touch etc.), faith-based films, movies & documentaries (e.g. Miracles from Heaven, War Room, Heaven Is for Real), music & record labels (e.g. Kirk Franklin, Tye Tribbett).

3. Publishing houses producing devotionals, books, and music.
4. Educational institutions: universities, Bible colleges, leadership schools, academies. (like Oral Roberts University, Liberty University, Covenant University).
5. Sales of different formats of devotionals, self-help books, and autobiographies
6. Hospitality businesses: Restaurants, hotels, or retail chains.
7. Real estate: Developing, buying, selling and renting of properties, housing estates commercial centres, events facilities
8. Corporate speaking engagements, leadership training, consulting, coaching services.
9. Networking with corporate sponsors, philanthropists, and wealthy believers.
10. Radio and TV stations generating ad revenue and selling airtime.
11. Bookstores, cafes, and investment firms.

D. **Ancillary Methods**: Finally, the wise steward wields legal structures with precision, leveraging advanced knowledge and financial wisdom, using tax and legal frameworks, to maximize financial benefits:
1. Non-profit organizations with clear governance.
2. Tax-exempt advantages according to the law.

3. Complex corporate entities designed to multiply and preserve wealth, while ensuring kingdom accountability.

Upright pastors who chose to access kingdom riches do not consume every morsel as manna in the wilderness, expecting overnight miracles. They recognize seasons, separate seed from bread, and sow again. They build with patience, guided not by pulpit theatrics but by proven principles and the whisper of the Spirit. Their abundance is neither magic nor accident, but the fruit of obedience, sacrifice, and kingdom stewardship.

When a kingdom citizen, pastor or layman, receives income or gift in monetary terms, let them hold fast to the same enduring principles: separate seed from bread, prepare the field, and sow deliberately, if they expect God's multiplying and exponential touch upon their seed.

Even if your field is ministry, do not consume all. For he who consumes like manna will always wait, scraping bowls for the next salary, the next offering, forever clutching at the fleeting hand-to-mouth provision. That's manna-like consumption.

Ministry is no excuse to neglect personal development, to ignore the sharpening of mind and tongue and spirit. Many church leaders focus only on spiritual growth, neglecting the need to become better speakers, better leaders, and more enterprising individuals. Such easily become stale to those weary souls who gather, hungry, hoping for treasures. Because spiritual graces and gifts open many to sycophancy, there is rarely any room for candid feedback from the pew to the pulpit, from the seat to the stage. Many folks may therefore continue to tolerate a preacher's excesses, struggling to make sense of their messages, and experiencing exhaustion instead of growth under their ministry.

Church leaders need to invest in personal growth. It is an essential step to take in the preliminary stages of your ministry. Let them sow into people, yes, but also into themselves, into the fields God has assigned them, becoming better communicators, wiser leaders, clearer thinkers, more excellent stewards.

Pastors can build significant wealth, even though it often sparks debates about the ethics of prosperity in ministry. While there are instances of financial mismanagement or exploitative practices, there are many preachers who acquire their wealth through means that are both godly and legitimate. Many have quietly followed the path of disciplined sowing, diligent reinvestment, and unrelenting personal development.

For a church leader who is focused solely on ministry with no inclination towards investment ventures, the same principles apply. Your fields are ripe with lives and you need to exchange real value if you expect to reap multiplied folds down the road. I am not talking about what you will reap hereafter, but what scriptural principles assure folks who comply without selective obedience. On days that are sunny, invest in yourself to offer more value. On days that are cloudy, exchange values that shape some lives and mould some others. Before the rain's first drop and until after the coming of the summer, sow some seeds. Pray for them, but that is not enough. Create value. Add value. Distribute value. Sow value on pinkish teenagers in college, on lily-like adults in their marriages. Invest value-filled counselling. Invest in guidance that extends value. Invest encouragements. Sow the seeds of time. Sow the seeds of money. Your sown seed is the value you create, the wisdom you invest in the tender hearts of teenagers, the strength you sow into marriages, the counsel you plant in the grief of widows, the prayers you offer when hope is hanging by a thread. Sow the seeds of your time, your insight, your learning, your comfort. Let the faint scent of your gift become a fragrance of life. Let the stumps and battered trees of wounded men and women bud again with hope because you chose not to hoard your seed. With the mere scent of talent, make unforgettable fragrance. With completely hewn-down trees, provide tangible hope of a budding again. From men of thistles and prickles, from women of weeds and wussies, don't cease to bring out precious treasures. In time, some will go away. Some will fade. Some will mock. But some will return, arms laden with fruit. Some will bring multiplied berries back into your life. That is your field. That is where you sow. And that is where, in due season, God will multiply and increase.

Whatever path you take, whether shepherding a congregation or journeying alongside as a faithful steward, your voyage into superabundance begins the very moment you choose to abide by the ancient protocols of financial wisdom woven into the fabric of Scripture.

This book has sought to uncover and lay bare these timeless principles in the clearest terms. The miracle of financial prosperity is stashed inside the seed you courageously separate and sow into your own field. Therefore, sow seed in your field. But do not ignore the King's portion; for that is the divine mystery that fertilizes your field in ways the best economists cannot decode nor the cleverest minds unravel. Start now. Start early. Because the quiet force of exponential increase needs time, time to root, time to sprout, time to overwhelm every barren patch of your existence with a harvest that defies human arithmetic.

Chapter 10

The Seed for Your Field: Your Escape Route

This is what it is—seed for your field. It is never meant for the altar, nor to be consumed. It is to be planted, either now or in the next season, guided by the wisdom of timing, the counsel of prudence, and the insight of the Spirit. For it is this seed, when sown in your field, that becomes the raw material for divine multiplication. And it is the multiplied portion that God magnifies in due season, to your astonishment and to His glory.

You can start sowing by learning a new skill, by refining an old one, by investing in yourself, your venture, your mission, your system. Sow by investing in a new venture, a system related to or outside of your primary job or venture. Sow by reinvesting profit, by expanding your capacity, by growing your outlets, by diversifying your streams. Sow by stretching into new territories, by pouring into new product lines, by venturing into virgin lands. This is sowing. This is how your seed germinates and becomes an orchard, not merely a loaf of bread.

Do not be deceived: it violates divine principle to haul all your seeds to the church or to your pastor, expecting God to multiply bread you have eaten on the altar. No, the Bible is clear. The King's portion is the part you give to the fellowship, the tithe, the offering, the mission, the outreach, the welfare, the charity, but that is not your seed sown in your field. The King's portion is the part that fertilizes your ground, that invites the rain. But it does not replace the seed.

By that divinely inspired formula, your total contribution to ecclesiastical offering, tithe, mission, outreach, building, welfare, charity donations and such like should not exceed twenty percent of your salary or profit – unless there is a special and urgent need which could arise once in a while!

Scripture gives us a formula that you can adopt if you are not very certain about what to do and how. Let your collective ecclesiastical giving not exceed a fifth of your earnings (salary or profit), except on rare occasions of urgent need, which could arise once in a while. Even then, let the urging be from the Holy Spirit, not the pulpit. Let such special donations be your choice, not someone else's compulsion. And once special needs are taken care of, it's good, godly, and practical to revert to that inspired blueprint.

Those who hide behind certain one-off instances in the Bible and repeatedly ask you to turn over your earnings are not being sincere with you. An urgent need can arise in the fellowship, and there can be a great course in the church, which may warrant a request for more than the recommended proportion; but when this happens, it is not imposed. Besides, such great courses and urgent needs are supposed to be on a once-in-a-while basis. It is only your church leader who smiles whenever you give grudgingly. Your pastor may smile at it without noticing the tenor of your disposition, but you sulk, your household groans, your field languishes barren, and God frowns at it.

When you keep turning over all you have to the church, you condemn yourself to merely surviving on layer-one supply, supply that comes in the morning, but leaves you in need by twilight. Promotion may come, bonuses may come, but you are still fetching from the same well, with a bigger bucket perhaps, but never building a river that flows with abundance. Don't be mystified. God commits Himself to multiplying ONLY sown seed, not bread eaten, not tears shed, not prayers chanted over barren soil.

Multiply zero by a thousand, and it remains zero. Raise zero seed to the power of one hundred and the result remains zero. Sow nothing and you reap nothing, no matter the leverage of gifts in your script and prophecies over your head. God respects His principle, and His principle compels Him to move on to the next-door field when there is nothing to multiply in yours. And He will graciously and justifiably multiply your compliant neighbour's enterprise every time He finds sown seeds in his field.

This is one reason many keep getting basic supplies, while few advance to the next levels of kingdom prosperity. This is the reason some rise and rise, while others remain stuck in the cycle of just enough. Your joyful giving is the rainfall that waters the seed, but the seed must be there in your field first. Otherwise, the heavens pour out abundance on empty soil, and you find yourself clinging to the next paycheck, the next prophetic push, the next fundraising rally, hoping. Do not deceive yourself. Sow in your field. Sow today. Sow tomorrow. That is the path from daily manna to perpetual multiplication, from survival to superabundance.

Giving to your church or pastor is not the same as sowing. That falls under the King's Portion, call it offering, sacrificial gift, covenant seed, alms, whatever name suits your creed. When Jesus told the parable of the sower, He said, "A sower went out to sow." Then He described the sower's field. Look again: the field was not the temple grounds or fellowship hall.

Christian giving is sacred, but it is not the same as sowing in your own field. One complements the other, but can never substitute it. Giving is not sowing. When you give, you receive, yes, but not necessarily the same substance. But when you sow into your field, you trigger the law of seedtime and harvest, convert your seed into a value carrier, and activate the power built into your seed to bring returns in folds of the value it carries. Then you can exchange value and experience the law of giving and receiving in full swing, with its promise of the correct worth (good measure) of the exchanged value. Exchange the same value with ten individuals and get the equivalence in return. That's a good and correct measure. You only start to grow riches as you exchange the same value with hundreds or thousands who equally trade in the correct monetary equivalence.

Giving earns you leverage, which could influence the incremental factor of what you sow. It fertilizes your soil. It draws heaven's rain. But none of these replaces seed sown in your own field. Almsgiving is not sowing. No! When you give to the poor, the Bible says you lend to God and He will pay you back (Prov. 19.17). Loan is not sowing. Loans earn you interest (where applicable) on repayment. But when you sow, you reap in folds augmented by the leverage of your giving.

Giving the King's portion is more than money. Those who truly understand the principle of giving the King's Portion know to give their time, expertise, services, products and other resources – not money only. But if you give all this and fail to separate and plant seed, you have only earned leverages that have no way of finding genuine expression without sown seeds. A fertilized ground without seed remains barren. Rain from heaven on an empty field produces nothing but weeds. Let your giving enrich your soil. But never let it substitute for seed in your own ground. That is how you rise from mere sustenance to overflowing abundance.

My Seed Voyage Experience

I began my seed voyage by first separating ten percent of my salary during my days as a banker. I quickly discovered there was scarcely any difference in my daily sustenance both before and after kick-starting that journey. After three months of faithfully carving out that ten percent, I raised the bar to twenty percent. If there was any strain, it came only from halting discretionary giving and spending, those little leaks that siphon destinies. By the time I began separating thirty percent, my wife, illuminated by the same light, began to save ten percent of hers.

Things became even more interesting once my wife embraced the principle. It helped us to set mutual goals for investment, steered our household towards prudence, and forged an unbreakable bond of accountability. We experimented with different savings options. We tried standing orders on every paycheck and thrift contributions with office colleagues. We attempted some other seed separation strategies that could be considered somewhat "crazy." We once even separated one hundred percent of my salary to seize a time-sensitive opportunity, leaning on my wife's salary for our immediate needs.

We started our investment expedition by investing in stocks and IPOs, harvesting mixed yields overall because some stocks went up while some others went down. We ventured into equity in a tech startup, but the company did not reach the stage of profitability before folding up. We invested in real estate using a loan that was tied to a percentage of our monthly salary, helping us to invest tomorrow's seed in today's opportunity. That became an unconscious seed savings approach because it automatically reduced the amount of money available for us to spend. These and some other investment strategies culminated in valuable experience for us.

When that loan was paid off, we sustained the discipline by automating a separation strategy to keep about that same percentage out of our reach, and it paid off.

That discipline built the bedrock of our first sawmill on an approximately 4,046 square meters plot, funded solely by separated seeds, even as our salaries continued. The sawmill was equipped with 6 machinery, including a Band-6 Head Saw – for cutting giant logs into slabs, cants, and large boards; a Circular Saw – for log cutting, rip cutting, crosscutting, re-sawing and trimming; and 4 other equipment.

A few years later, after gathering a new set of seed streams from different quarters, we opened a chicken processing factory–which employed nine people. Afterwards, we progressed by starting an IT firm co-founded with a trusted friend, at which point I resigned my banking job while my wife continued hers. Her salaried job kept providing seed and bread, a layer 1 supply. I was also placed on salary, much less than my last salary as a banker, also at the same layer. But then, we had access to 2nd layer supplies through the businesses.

Those separated seeds from the first layer of God's provision have since grown into multiplied seeds at the second layer, far beyond what the first layer could ever offer. Each cycle, each seed, became living proof that God's covenant of multiplication stands true wherever you plant, from Lagos to London, from New Delhi to New Orleans.

Placate Present Cravings or Feed Future Possibilities

Placate present cravings, or feed the boundless horizon of future possibilities. This is the solemn choice that stands before every soul entrusted with the gift of income. I know that the drumbeat of daily needs and regular desires echoes loudly in your ears. Yes, the sweet siren-call of instant pleasures whispers sweet and nigh. I don't dispute that everywhere is filled with very loud distractions, each one urging you to spend, to consume, to live for momentary applause. Yet, hidden within the folds of patience and discipline lies this wisdom, a principle that transforms the ordinary into the extraordinary. It urges every income generator: Wait. Hold back. Separate your seed and invest, for tomorrow carries treasures that today's hungry hands cannot yet grasp.

Your present income, stable and sure, might look like a continuously streaming well, gushing steadily to quench today's thirst only. It often comes with burning cravings and seductive whispers of instant gratification. The immediate urge is to let it pour freely on the pleasures of today, a lavish meal, a fleeting indulgence, a new gadget gleaming in store windows, a designer cloth that catches the light just so, or that exotic vacation beckoning from glossy travel magazines. But the burning cravings never hint that immediate gratification leaves you with a tomorrow unguarded, a future allotted to despair. Those seductive whispers never give any inkling that true financial wisdom lies not in how much you earn, but in how intelligently you transform those earnings into engines of lasting prosperity.

What if instead, you could build your well into a flowing river that grows deeper and wider with time and in phases? What if, once you arrive in the days of your river, you could guide it to carve valleys of abundance through the parched fields of life? What if some of it flows freely for immediate nourishment, with another portion dammed to further generate power for the future of your tomorrow? This is the essence of separating your seed, a deliberate act of restraint that builds the foundation for future abundance.

A deliberate act of restraint is not an act of denial; it's a reimagining of priorities. It's based on the understanding that the joy of a single "today" can be multiplied into the bliss of countless tomorrows. It's the understanding that every dollar, every seed, that graces your hand holds the power to either strand or to swell. It's the recognition that every dollar you earn carries within it a choice–to be consumed in the fleeting present or transformed into a soldier in your army of future wealth creation. Every small portion you separate for sowing builds a foundation for brighter days ahead. When you separate your seed, when you save a portion of your earnings, you are not merely setting aside money; you are preparing the seeds of boundless possibilities, seeds that, when nurtured, can grow into forests of opportunity. Those seeds become your investments that have the potential to generate extra income. The extra income generated from your investments is not just money; it is the gateway to freedom, the freedom to choose, to dream, and to live fulfilling the essence of life.

Those who align with these principles transform the fickle coin of the present into an army that wages war for their future. They plant trees whose fruits will one day nourish generations and whose shade will shelter their children from scorching seasons. They look beyond the gleam of new gadgets, the allure of designer labels, and the siren song of glossy travel brochures. Instead, they choose to invest, patiently, wisely, deliberately, in ventures that bloom beyond their sight, in businesses that rise like towering oaks after rain, into ideas that break forth like rivers long dammed by neglect and inaction.

This is the way of the seed voyager: the path of waiting, of diligence, of transforming today's careful restraint into tomorrow's unshackled freedom. It is the way of turning income into seed, and seed into harvest, and harvest into forests of enduring abundance. It is the way of refusing to live merely for today's applause, while quietly building an inheritance of blessings that will echo into a lasting legacy.

Investing is the bridge between saving and abundance. It is the act of placing your resources into ventures that can innovate, grow, and thrive. Startups, with their bold ideas and untapped potential, offer a chance to be part of something transformative. System-based investments, with their structured and often automated approaches, provide a steady path to growth. But, like any journey, investing requires research, patience, and a willingness to embrace risk. It is not a gamble, but a calculated step toward financial freedom.

In today's age of entrepreneurial renaissance, well-researched businesses and startups bloom like wildflowers after spring rain. They offer fertile ground for those willing to plant their financial seeds wisely. These ventures, selected with careful deliberation and due diligence, can transform modest investments into streams of passive income that flow long after your initial efforts have been forgotten.

System-based investments, whether automated stock portfolios, real estate trusts, or well-structured business models, offer frameworks for your financial garden to grow with minimal daily tending. Like a well-designed irrigation system, they can distribute your resources efficiently while you focus on your primary income source.

I know that the path of delayed gratification is not strewn with roses. It is never paved with comfort. It demands grit to watch others indulge while you invest. It demands courage to trust in tomorrow while today beckons seductively. But in this lies the power of the time-tested principles: every luxury forgone plants a seed for future harvest; every fleeting thrill denied becomes the cornerstone of lasting abundance; and every impulsive purchase resisted now becomes capital in your arsenal of wealth creation.

The beauty of delayed gratification lies in its ripple effect. When you choose to save and invest, you are not just securing your own future; you are contributing to a larger ecosystem. Your investments fuel innovation, create jobs, and drive progress. They become a testament to the power of patience and the rewards of foresight.

When you look at your salary, see not just compensation for today's labour, but also the raw material and seed for tomorrow's dreams. Let your earnings be more than mere numbers that flash briefly in your bank account before vanishing into the ether of daily expenses. Hold back a portion, not as a sacrifice, but as a gift to your future self. Invest those seeds in ventures that resonate with your values and aspirations. And as you do, watch as the seeds you plant today transform into building blocks of future abundance. For in the end, the art of waiting is the art of living fully; not just for today, but for all the days yet to come.

In the voyage of financial seed, those who master the art of strategic restraint often find themselves leading the race of wealth creation. Their patience becomes their power, and their foresight, their fortune. So next time your earnings arrive, pause before the spending spree. Ask yourself: will this impulsive purchase feed my future, or merely satisfy my present?

Handling Seed for Your Field

Your seed is sacred. It is the marrow of your mandate, the divine instrument entrusted into your hands for the fulfilment of destiny with prosperity. You cannot toss it about like breadcrumbs to passing birds, nor treat its holy instructions as mere suggestions. A careless sower reaps loss. Sow your seed anywhere–it could be trampled underfoot, it could be scorched by the sun, it could be choked by thorns! That is not stewardship, but negligence. You must take your own seed as a major component of the resources deployed for the fulfilment of your life's mandate. God hands you seed as proof of His covenant to provide for your journey and empower the mandate stamped upon your life.

Your seed possesses its own life. You can grow it into a mighty oak, able to provide a much needed shade for an entire community. That oak could develop into a forest capable of feeding a nation. You can transition your forest into a fortress, sufficient to profit your generation with surplus for the next generation. You hold the future in your hands when you hold your seed. Handle it with fear, with reverence, with unwavering focus, for it is the leverage of heaven upon your earthly assignment.

Every seed is significant to your journey. But a consumed seed is a covenant squandered. Every consumed seed sinks the eater into the trench of poverty, inch by inch. A seed merely separated but left unsown keeps the voyager stagnant, forever circling the same weary mountain of unfulfilled potential. But a seed sown, deliberately, prayerfully, and wisely, lifts the voyager up on the ladder of prosperity, one step at a time.

Neglect your seed, and you undermine the principles that unlock the second and third layers of divine provision. Scatter your seed in every random field, and you may watch your labour rot in soil unworthy of your sacrifice. Lose your seed; you forfeit the most crucial element of your journey and auto-reroute to an undesirable destination. Eat your seed, and you join the long, hopeless queue of those whose stories expire before their legacy even begins.

Let us pause and consider the diverse workings of the seed you separate from your supply.

Seed Kept (saved) for Your Field (For Your Escape)

It may seem obvious that once you separate your seed, you must sow it at once. But it is rarely that simple. Between separation and sowing, there is often the vital period of keeping it safe. There are pressing reasons to keep your seed in safe custody before planting.

i. When your seed is not enough for sowing, you must gather until it becomes enough to launch your next venture, like saving for premises, equipment, or start-up capital.

ii. When the sowing season has not arrived, you store your seed. Perhaps your venture requires legal approvals, operational licenses, or staff recruitment and training before you can truly plant.

iii. Your seed may need to be in savings mode when your field (or venture) is not yet ready. Examples include a farmland that requires ploughing, a product prototype that requires modification before mass production, a venture that requires patent registration, a website, equipment importation and installation and such like, before actual operations.

iv.   When your field is not ready, your seed must wait. Maybe the ground needs ploughing, or your prototype requires perfecting before mass production, or your equipment needs installation before the work begins.

Seed Saving Warnings: Preparing the Escape Routes

I have learned through the crucible of experience that while saving your seed is already a narrow path paved with thorns, there is yet another equally narrow, possibly more slippery, path. It is the ability and discipline to guard your saved seed for its appointed sowing. This is where many falter, where discipline is tested in the furnace of hunger, distraction, and enticing alternatives.

What are the holes?

i.   Seeds kept in custody can be diverted to other uses.
ii.   Seeds kept can be eaten (during hunger, lack, or cravings).
iii.   Seeds improperly kept can get spoilt.
iv.   Seeds improperly kept can be stolen.

Beware. Guard it with vigilance. For every seed saved is a future harvest in waiting, but only if it is sown in its season.

Practical Ways to Save and Separate Your Seed

Many stumble at this very first gate of abundance. Many find the culture of savings very difficult to imbibe. It is not surprising, for the world clamours ceaselessly, enticing the hand to spend, to scatter every hard-earned gain upon fleeting pleasures and pressing needs. Yet savings is not merely a wise suggestion; it is a divine principle, woven into the fabric of God's promise to multiply only the seed you separate and sow.

If your hands tremble in the early days of this voyage, so much so that separating your seed is proving very difficult, you are not alone. Many have felt the strain of denying the present to secure the future. But there are practical, everyday methods, simple yet potent, that can help you save more, build your seed reserve, and prepare for the harvest God Himself has ordained. Let us explore them together.

1) Standing Order Savings: Set up a standing order that moves a fixed portion of your salary into a separate savings account the moment you get paid. This is one of the simplest and most effective ways to build a disciplined savings culture. It puts extra cash out of sight, starves the ever-hungry hand of spending, and forces you to grow accustomed to living on less while building your seed reserve without thinking.

2) Rotational Savings Scheme: This is called Susu or Ajo (in West Africa), or Partner Savings Scheme (in the Caribbean): This communal savings method lets you contribute a fixed amount,

weekly or monthly, into a pool shared by trusted friends, with each member in the scheme taking turns to collect the whole sum in predetermined rotation. To illustrate a rotational savings scheme, consider a savings group with three friends, Ann, Bridget, and Christie. This group decides that each member would contribute a sum of $1000 to a monthly pool, totalling $3000 per month, with a termination period of one rotation. And to make things easier, these friends decide that the pay-out rotation will happen alphabetically, from A to C. This setup implies that Ann would receive $3000 at the end of the first month, Bridget at the end of the second, and Christie at the end of the third. Afterwards, they will cancel the contribution scheme, since they set a termination period for one rotation. The scheme cycle can continue until a second or third round if the group determines so.

3) Credit Cooperative Society Contribution: A workplace or community credit cooperative society contribution scheme works on the principle of mutual benefit. Members join voluntarily and contribute monthly into a collective pot that cycles lump sums among members, funds projects, offers dividends, contributes through membership fees, shares, or regular contributions towards and offers savings and loans services to members. The members take turns accessing a lump sum, which can be used for projects or investments, and also receive benefits such as lower prices, dividends, or specialized services at reduced costs. Profit or surplus generated by the cooperative is reinvested in the cooperative or

distributed among members based on their contributions or usage of services. The scheme fosters community growth, protects your seed from impulse spending, and unlocks access to pooled resources.

4) Collective Investment Fund: Gather with others to make fixed, regular contributions into a shared investment fund. It holds every member accountable and pools strength to access bigger opportunities that might be beyond their individual reach.

5) Payroll Deductions Savings: This is an automated, employer-facilitated, tax-efficient, direct savings mechanism. It allows you to set up automated arrangements with your employer to transfer a portion of your paycheck into a separate savings or investment account, forcing disciplined financial planning. You save before you see the money, ensuring tomorrow is secured before today makes its demands.

6) Save Your Raise Strategy: Whenever your income increases or you receive bonuses, keep living on your previous salary. This is a global cultural and psychological savings approach to surplus money in which you set aside monetary gifts, salary increases, upfront bonuses, or tax refunds. Since you are already accustomed to living on your previous income, this is an easy way to direct the difference into savings, so your seed grows without your lifestyle swelling to swallow it up.

7) Pay Yourself First Approach: A disciplined approach to personal finance in which immediate allocation of "non-negotiable" 10-30%

of your paycheck is automatically transferred into a saving or investment account immediately after getting paid, before expenses and discretionary spending. It is the salary you pay your future before any other bill takes its share.

8) Envelope Cash-Based Budgeting System: A tangible budget management tactic in which you physically separate your money into labelled envelopes for different spending categories (e.g., rent, groceries, investment, entertainment, transportation and emergency funds). Once the cash in an envelope is spent, you cannot spend more in that category until the next budget cycle. This method is widely used in many countries to control unnecessary spending while prioritizing savings.

9) Dollar-Cost Averaging: This approach is commonly used in US, Europe, and Asia; enabling you to consistently invest a fixed amount in stocks, ETFs, or cryptocurrency every month, with minimum investments as low as $10 or $15 monthly. It reduces risk and builds long-term wealth with no need to time the market. It is also similar to the Middle Eastern Zakat-inspired Savings, a principle of setting aside a fixed percentage starting at a minimum of 2.5% of income for savings.

10) Piggy Banking Method or Small Change Savings: A micro-saving approach in which daily loose change or small bills are saved in a piggy bank or jar. It feels small but adds up to surprising sums in the long run, ready to be sown into bigger ventures once full. Once the jar is full, you can then deposit the money into savings or investment

account. This method is popular in many cultures and is a simple way to build savings gradually.

11) 52-Week Incremental Saving Challenge (Global): Start by saving $1 the first week, $2 the second, $3 the third, up to $52 by week fifty-two. It feels effortless, but yields $1,378 in a year. This method is popular in many countries for building savings gradually, and can be customized for monthly or bi-weekly salary earners.

12) Monthly Incremental Savings: Start with 1% of your income saved in month one. Add another 1% every month. By year's end, you'll be saving 12% monthly, without feeling overwhelmed from day one.

13) Divide your income into separate accounts for expenses, discretionary spending, and savings. Automate the transfers so your seed is locked away before your desires even know it has arrived. For instance,

- One account is for fixed expenses (rent, bills).
- One account is for discretionary spending.
- One account is for savings and investments.

Set up automatic transfers to these separate accounts as soon as you receive your salary. This ensures that a portion of your income is saved before you can spend it. Many countries use this method to encourage regular savings.

14) Gold or Precious Metals Savings: A tangible asset savings strategy in the (Middle East and Asia) countries like India, China and the UAE, where you regularly buy small amounts of gold or silver as a

form of savings, long-term financial security, and hedge against inflation. Gold, being a tangible asset, can be liquidated when needed and often appreciates in value with time.

15) Fixed Deposit Savings: This is a common scheme in countries like India, Nigeria, UAE, and UK. Lock funds into fixed deposits or term deposit accounts for a set period at higher interest. Early withdrawal is penalized, so you protect your seed while it grows in a safe corner.

1. Micro-Investing Apps: In USA, Europe, Asia, apps like Acorns, Stash, or Bamboo help build wealth passively by automatically investing spare change from everyday purchases into stocks, ETFs, or mutual funds. With this strategy, you can grow your seed stealthily, without fuss or elaborate planning.
2. "Save the Difference" Strategy: Whenever you save money on a purchase (e.g., through discounts, coupons, or price comparisons), transfer the difference to your savings account. For example, if you save $10 on groceries, move that $10 into savings immediately.
3. Zero-Based Budgeting: Allocate every dollar of your income a task, including savings. No leftovers for wasteful whims. Everything is directed with precision and purpose.
4. Festive or Seasonal Savings: Save specifically for festivals, holidays, or seasonal events. Open a separate savings account for these occasions and contribute a small amount regularly. This prevents financial stress during celebrations and helps you avoid debt or dipping a hand in your investment savings.

5. Mandatory Personal Development Fund: Regularly set aside a fixed percentage for skill development. This helps you to invest in courses and certifications gradually, increase future earning potential and achieve the dual benefit of savings and personal growth.

These methods are not magic. They are proven, battle-tested shields against the endless calls of instant consumption. Adopt one or two, combine them, or adapt them to your context. Whatever you do, protect your seed. Nurture it. And one day, your forest will stand tall for generations to admire.

1. **Seed Sown**

Let me remind you again: only the seed you sow, never the one you consume, can activate God's multiplying and exponential powers into your story. As the season of planting draws near, tend your field with diligence. Prepare your venture, your ground, your terrain, so it becomes a fertile cradle for your seed, able to nourish, protect, and sustain it through its silent seasons. Once buried in the obscurity of soil, your seed will wrestle with its first hurdles, slowly cracking open their outer layer and the unseen resistance of the dark earth. Yet, in due time, by the mysterious working of divine laws, the seed will transmute, sprout fragile shoots, then bloom and blossom into a living testimony. It is there, in the quiet perseverance of sown seed, that God's power is activated, birthing fruit, multiplying provision, and bringing sustenance not just for you, but for the many who will someday eat from the harvest of your field.

Chapter 11

All Seeds Are not equal

All seeds are not created equal. Some carry within them the power of perennial return, offering lasting, season-upon-season fruitfulness that far surpasses the yield of their fleeting cousins. Some seeds demand more of you: more patience, more nurturing, more sacrifice. Some break the earth in mere months, offering quick blossoms that fade just as swiftly. Others tarry in hidden places, taking years to bear their first fruit; yet, when they do, they anchor forests and fortresses that outlast generations. In the same way, not all ventures, not all investments, are of equal weight or worth. Each field differs in its promise, each opportunity unique in its performance, its potential, and the kinds of harvest it offers.

Check out this exciting verse from the opening chapter of the Holy Bible:

> **And God said, Behold, I have given you every herb bearing seed, which is upon the face of the earth, and every tree, in the which is the fruit of a tree yielding seed; to you it shall be for meat**
> **Gen 1:29 (KJV)**

Take a closer look at this sacred verse, and you will discover a profound truth woven into its lines: God gives us two kinds of seed. First, the *herb-bearing seed*, quick to sprout, quick to yield, nourishing for a season. And then, He gives us the *tree-yielding seed*, steadfast, resilient, destined to tower over fields and endure through generations. Read the verse again, and let your spirit grasp this mystery: not all seeds are alike, and each carries a different measure of God's intent and promise.

> **And God said, Behold, I have given you every herb bearing seed, which is upon the face of the earth, and every tree, in the which is the fruit of a tree yielding seed; to you it shall be for meat**
> **Gen 1:29 (KJV)**

The theme is heavy with spiritual and financial gravity. Its scope is vast, and its depth is profound. That God placed it in the very first chapter of the Bible, before Adam was created or brought into the garden, was with intention. The function of herbs is utterly different from that of trees. Herbs serve immediate, temporal needs; trees anchor generations. Both are gifts granted to every man as part of God's solemn supply. But woe to the man who consumes his seed with his bread, for he will never witness the sprouting of his potential herbs or the blossoming of his towering but never-to-be trees. He robs himself of the marvels of multiplication and the legacy of exponential upsurge.

You may eat roots and herbs, and savour the leaves and fruits of your trees, but if you fail to preserve and sow the seed, you leave your field barren for weeds alone to claim.

Herb-bearing seeds and tree-yielding seeds differ in life span, growth cycle, reproductive strategies, and generational impact. Likewise, the venture into which you sow your seed determines whether it will be short-lived like herbs or enduring like trees.

Herb-bearing Seed

These are seeds that have the drive, resources, and mandate to complete their life cycle in one or two growing seasons cycle quickly. They sprout and take root, grow leaves and stems, bear flowers and develop fruits within a season or two, then fade. They thrive on speed and responsiveness, adapting to rapid shifts in terrain. Likewise, short-term ventures thrive in fleeting windows, turning trends into quick harvests. They require sharp reflexes and readiness to pivot, not long roots. The following characteristics of herbs will help you understand the nature of herb-bearing seeds and give you hints on how to plan and prepare your short-term business ventures:

a. **Lifespan**: They germinate, grow, flower, set seed, and die within one or two growing seasons.
b. **Growth Cycle**: They typically have a rapid growth cycle, with quick germination, flowering, and seed production.
c. **Reproductive Strategy**: They invest much of their energy into producing seeds within a short timeframe to ensure the survival of the next generation.

d. **Adaptations**: They naturally adapt to habitats with shorter growing seasons or more variable environmental conditions.

Short-Term Business Ventures: Like herb-bearing plants, these businesses typically have a relatively quick turnaround time, often focused on meeting a specific demand or capitalizing on a fleeting trend. These ventures often require agility, market awareness, and the ability to adapt quickly to changing circumstances to maximize profitability within a short timeframe.

Here are some examples:

i. Pop-up shops: Setting up temporary retail spaces to sell seasonal or trendy products, such as holiday-themed items or limited-edition merchandise.

ii. ii. Event planning services: Offering services to plan and execute events like weddings, corporate gatherings, or festivals on a contract basis.

iii. Seasonal businesses: Operating businesses that cater to seasonal demands, such as a snow removal and ploughing service in winter, Christmas-related products and services, Fireworks sales for New Year's Eve and Independence Day, or a beach gear rental service in summer.

iv. Freelance or gig economy work: Providing services such as graphic design, writing, programming, or consulting on a project-by-project basis through platforms like Upwork, Fiverr, or TaskRabbit.

v. Dropshipping: Creating an online store and selling products without holding inventory. When a product is sold, the supplier ships it directly to the customer, reducing upfront costs and risks.

vi. Social media influencer/content creator: Building a personal brand and leveraging social media platforms to promote products or services through sponsored posts, affiliate marketing, or product placements.

vii. Seasonal agricultural ventures: Planting and harvesting crops with short growing seasons, such as micro-greens, specialty herbs, or certain fruits and vegetables.

viii. Mobile car washing/detailing: Providing on-demand car washing or detailing services at customers' locations, catering to busy individuals or events like car shows.

Tree-yielding Seed:

Tree-yielding Seeds are different: slow to mature but mighty when established. They have the in-built obligation, ability, and fuel to grow stronger year after year, and bear flowers and fruits for several seasons after growth. Their roots go deep; their canopies stretch wide over the years. Such are the long-term ventures: manufacturing empires, real estate portfolios, technology firms with lasting impact, energy projects that fuel generations, schools that shape futures. They demand patience, resilience, strategic nurturing, and the faith to weather dormant winters until the day comes when their branches bear fruit year after year.

   a. Lifespan: They live for multiple years or even decades, depending on species, often standing on or re-growing from the same roots or base each year.
   b. Growth Cycle: They have a slower growth cycle and even periods of dormancy during adverse conditions, often taking longer to establish themselves and bear fruit.
   c. Reproductive Strategy: They often allocate energy differently, investing in growing strong root systems and storage organs in order to survive adverse conditions and regrow in subsequent years.
   d. Adaptation: They inhabit more stable environments and develop mechanisms to survive across multiple years, such as the ability to store energy reserves or resist freezing temperatures.

Long-Term Business Ventures

Long-term business ventures typically involve sustained efforts and investments over an extended period, aiming for lasting success and stability. These ventures require strategic planning, sustainable business models, and ongoing adaptation to changing market conditions to achieve long-term viability and success. There are some examples below:

i. Manufacturing: Establishing a company that produces goods, such as automobiles, electronics, or consumer packaged goods, with a focus on long-term production, distribution, and market presence.

ii. ii. Real estate development: Investing in the acquisition, construction, and management of properties for residential, commercial, or industrial purposes, aiming for long-term appreciation and rental income.

iii. Franchising: Building a network of franchise locations for a proven business concept, such as fast-food restaurants, hotels, or retail stores, with a focus on expanding market share and brand recognition with time.

iv. Technology startups: Developing innovative products or services in sectors like software, biotechnology, or clean energy, with the goal of long-term growth, market leadership, and potentially disruptive impact.

v. Healthcare services: Establishing clinics, hospitals, or specialized medical facilities to provide long-term care, diagnostic services, or treatment options in response to ongoing healthcare needs.

vi. Education institutions: Founding schools, colleges, or training centers to offer educational programs and services, aiming to foster lifelong learning and personal development within communities.

vii. Energy projects: Investing in renewable energy infrastructure, such as solar farms, wind turbines, or hydroelectric plants, to provide sustainable energy solutions over the Long-term.

viii. Consumer goods brands: Building a brand identity and portfolio of products in industries like apparel, cosmetics, or home goods, with a focus on customer loyalty and market longevity.

ix. Infrastructure projects: Participating in the planning, financing, and construction of large-scale infrastructure projects, such as highways, bridges, or public transportation systems, to support economic development and improve quality of life over generations.

x. Investment management: Providing financial services such as asset management, wealth planning, or retirement planning, with a focus on long-term wealth accumulation and preservation for clients.

Herb-Bearing vs Tree-Yielding Enterprises

In the divine economy of seed and harvest, not all ventures are created equal. *Herb-bearing* (short-term) Ventures and *Tree-yielding* (long-term) Enterprises are worlds apart in their nature, their demands, and their destinies:

a. **Time Horizon**: The herb-bearing venture is like the fast-sprouting shoot that springs up swiftly, flourishes for a season, and soon withers away. It yields quick returns, short-lived gains, and immediate satisfaction. It thrives in short cycles, seizing passing winds of short-lived opportunities and the transient sun of trends. Its horizon is immediate profit; its heartbeat, quick returns. It leaps at fleeting trends, seeking swift harvests while the season lasts. The tree-yielding enterprise, however, takes time to sprout, demands patience and tending, but in its fullness, it towers strong, offering shade, fruit, and legacies that endure beyond a single season. Its roots burrow deep into the soil, anchoring against tempests, drawing unseen strength. Its horizon is generational. It seeks enduring profit, not just for today, but for decades. It labours to build market longevity, brand reputation, and unshakable customer loyalty that will outlive those who first tended its shoots.

b. **Goals and Objectives**: In goals and objectives, the herb-bearing venture craves instant fruit. It is opportunistic, thriving on the pulse of the moment, seeking the spoils of temporary niches, eager to capitalize on the fickleness of markets. The tree-yielding enterprise sets its sights higher and further. It plants for legacy. It seeks not only profit, but stature, dominance, and the slow, steady compounding of reputation into renown.

c. **Strategy and Planning**: Herb-bearing businesses typically employ reactive or opportunistic strategies, seizing immediate opportunities or addressing immediate challenges without extensive long-term planning. Tree-yielding businesses employ strategic planning processes that consider market trends, competitive landscapes, and internal capabilities to develop sustainable business models and competitive advantages. In strategy and planning, herb-bearing ventures often scramble, pivot, and react with quick steps and uncalculated risks, chasing immediate opportunities or addressing immediate challenges. But tree-yielding enterprises lay out pathways in advance, charting maps that take into account valleys and mountains yet unseen, considering market trends, competitive landscapes, and internal capabilities; as well as designing models that can withstand seasons of drought and storms alike.

d. **Risk Management**: In risk, the herb-bearing venture gambles, willing to take higher risks in pursuit of short-term gains. It trades security for the tantalizing promise of fast reward. But the tree-yielding enterprise weighs each risk against the far horizon, thinking in terms of generations, not quarters. It is prudent, planned, and measured, knowing that roots take time and branches must be strong enough to bear the weight of many harvests.

v. **Investment and Resource Allocation**: In investment and resource allocation, herb-bearing ventures pour resources into now, seeking quick conversion of seed into immediate profitability. Tree-yielding enterprises invest in unseen roots: infrastructure, research, innovation, human capital. They sow in quiet seasons, preparing for the glorious spread of branches that will one day cast shade over entire markets.

vi. **Customer Relationships**: Where customer relationships are concerned, herb-bearing ventures are transactional, eager for sales, gratified with the once-off exchange. But tree-yielding enterprises court their customers like stewards of a vineyard, tending each vine with care, seeking not just to satisfy, but to build a relationship whose fruit ripens over a lifetime.

vii. **Adaptability and Flexibility**: And while herb-bearing ventures are agile and swift to turn, darting with every wind of change, tree-yielding enterprises balance adaptability with unshakable resolve. They bend, but they do not break. They adapt, but they do not uproot. They grow taller, stronger, and fuller with each passing season.

Thus, it is that not all seeds are equal, and not all ventures are the same. Some feed you for a day; others build legacies that echo for generations. Choose your field. Choose your seed. Choose your season.

Should a starter pursue short-term or long-term ventures?

The path of a starter is fraught with questions, some subtle, others loud enough to rattle your bones, especially at that crucial time when dreams are blazing and the world seems to feel infinite. But no question seems more vital than this: should you build for the instant—an herb for swift harvest, or for the long haul—an oak for the ages? Should you create a quick, vibrant sketch that captures the moment, or craft a masterpiece that unfolds over years?

Both short-term and long-term business ventures hold their own magic, their own promises, and their own rewards.

The short-term path glitters with immediate possibilities, a thrilling blaze that sparks confidence and hones your craft. It is a field of fast failures and quick lessons. It offers the thrill of express execution, fast feedback, rapid returns, and the chance to pivot as you grow. You can ride current market trends, solve immediate problems, and potentially reap swift rewards. This path is for the bold experimenter, eager to test the waters and refine their craft. Such ventures teach invaluable lessons at a fast pace, allowing you to fail fast, learn faster, and pivot with agility. For starters, it is a training ground where risk is measured, and rewards can really build confidence. It is perfect for testing your entrepreneurial wings without committing your entire life's journey to a single path.

But then, there is the oak—the long-term venture that demands patience, vision, and the audacity to believe in tomorrow's forest while tending today's fragile sapling. It is a marathon, not a sprint, requiring roots to dig deep before the stems and the fruits appear. This type of business often tackles deeper problems, builds stronger foundations, and creates lasting value that compounds with time. A long-term venture is not for the faint-hearted but for those with resilience and foresight. They give you the chance to build something truly meaningful, something that offers the ultimate reward, to leave a legacy that outlives your initial dreams. This is the business that becomes a household name, the startup that grows into an empire, the venture that carries enduring impact.

Yet, neither path is inherently better. The beauty lies in understanding that this choice is not about better or worse – it's about alignment with your current season of life. The choice lies in your goals and temperament, and what season your heart truly beats for. Do you crave quick wins to learn and grow, or are you ready to commit to the slow, steady burn? Are you in a season of experimental growth, ready to test and learn rapidly? Or are you prepared to sink deep roots and nurture the evolution of something monumental that might take years to fully bloom?

One thing is sure: many long-term successes are born from short-term ventures that evolved, eventually. Short-term ventures can fund long-term dreams. Long-term ventures can spawn short-term opportunities. The two paths are not mutually exclusive but complementary notes in your entrepreneurial masterpiece. The starter's journey is one of exploration, where each step teaches, and each venture shapes the next.

So, dream boldly, but choose based on your resources, your risk tolerance, and most importantly, your heart's calling. This is because, whether it is a sprint or a marathon, success in this voyage comes to those who pour their full passion into their chosen path.

Your strategic investment is the field. Your intentional effort is the sowing. The real masterpiece, whether from a herb bearing seed or a tree yielding seed, awaits your first bold move. Dare to choose and dare to shine. The world awaits your brilliance.

The Channels of Value Exchange - Where Sown Seed Aids Escape

God never funds laziness or ignorance. He empowers stewards: those who can search for value in the various channels of abundance where they can sow and expect God's incremental power to do its work.

There are a few gates to value exchange which, if you knock correctly with your separated seeds, can open you up to a consistent flow of abundance. Those who do not understand these gates often spiritualize their way into scarcity. But if you master them, you won't chase money, money will recognize your value and chase you instead. If your complaint is about zero or low income, this is your wake-up call to mine what God has already placed within and around you.

1st Channel: People (Money Moves in Flesh and Blood)

You prayed for money. God sent people. He does not send a cheque, not a bank alert, not miracle money, but people. You asked for increase; He brought relationships. It walks in on two legs, wrapped in human skin. It shows up through a phone call, through a stranger's recommendation. God's response walks in through the boss you resent, the vendor you overlooked, the connection you misjudged. You cried for a breakthrough; He introduced you to someone: a neighbour, a colleague, a stranger online. But because the package didn't look like the prayer, you missed the provision. You allowed pride, blindness, or busyness to build a wall between you and your answer. That's how several people stay broke: misreading divine strategy for random interaction.

Look around; every divine deposit you need for your next financial shift is trapped in someone God has already introduced to your life. But your magic-seeking-mind ignored them, or mislabelled them, or failed to manage them. You didn't steward the relationship. You didn't discern the destiny link. You didn't learn how to serve, how to solve, or how to stay visible enough for others to remember your name when opportunity knocks.

Let's be clear: money moves in people. It wears human skin. It lives in phone numbers you haven't dialled a year, in messages you forgot to reply, in friends you cut off too early, and in mentors you never listened to. Some carry keys. Others carry doors. A few of them are the very doors you've all the while been praying for.

People are currency.

Some carry access. Others carry insight. A few carry platforms. Many carry pain, and if you can solve their pain, they'll pay you for it.

God has a vault called "men." And money is often buried in their problems, plans, priorities, or even their pain. It's your job to unearth it by creating value, distributing help, being unforgettable, or becoming indispensable.

You're not broke if you carry value. You're just undiscovered.

And maybe… untrained in the sacred art of relational wealth.

This is not flattery. It's not motivational gibberish. It's spiritual, psychological, and practical truth: God often hides treasure in men. Not just in prophets or relatives, but also in clients, colleagues, customers, critics, friends, and even enemies. Every man carries something. Every woman holds a measure of value. And if you learn to honour, observe, serve, and solve problems around people, your wallet will start reflecting it.

The real money is not always in hard skills or hard work. Sometimes, it's in human networks. That's why the broke man with access can become a bridge to fortune, and the skilled man with pride can remain stuck in obscurity.

Do you know how many lives have changed simply because someone mentioned their name in the right room?

- That woman who got a job because someone remembered her smile during a volunteer event.
- That man who got a million-dollar contract because he helped someone with a ride three years earlier.
- That struggling baker who now ships across the country because an old classmate shared her cake photo on social media.

Listen: you are one person away from a financial shift. But here's the twist; that person, no matter how strategically placed, won't help you if you have no seed sown, no value to exchange, nothing to offer. That person (though a supposed link to your long-awaited answer) won't remember you if you burn every bridge with your careless attitude, or keep playing small, in the hope that someone will "just discover you."

Relationships are currencies. Some people are like open doors: walk through and you are established for success. Others are locked chests: solve them and you unlock overflowing riches. Some are wells: serve them and draw from their depth for years of refreshing flow. A few are gates: honour them, and they'll swing you open to a life of global impact.

But you will not profit from any of them if you walk around like everyone owes you something.

You must carry value; not drama, not entitlement, not spiritual pride.

You must carry real value: the kind that meets a need, solves a problem, adds delight, relieves pressure, or creates momentum.

The people God sends are not always wealthy. Some are broke today, but will fund nations tomorrow. Some are awkward now, but will become industry giants. You must learn to build genuine friendships and plant seeds of service and goodwill in people; not for gain, but because it's the right thing to do. But guess what? Money follows those who build value-rich relationships, every time.

If you're broke, don't just pray louder. Get into rooms. Volunteer. Connect. Collaborate. Recommend others. Send that message. Follow up. Serve someone who can't pay you back today. Honour people even when it's inconvenient. Be visible in ways that leave fragrance, not frustration.

You may be good with ideas, but someone else has the audience. You may have the skill, but another has the structure. You may have the product, but some persons have the platform.

Alone, you may remain invisible; but together, you multiply wealth.

It's not manipulative to be strategic with people. It's wise. This is not about using people; it's about honouring the presently visible and invisible treasures God placed in them. This is not chasing money; it's cultivating access through service. This is not being fake; it's being fruitful.

The poor isolate themselves, thinking they're "guarding their peace." The wise draw close to those who carry grace, strength, light, and leverage. If Jesus walked with 12 men for impact, who are you walking with for increase?

And if you truly want to unlock the abundance in people, learn these three postures:

- Presence – Show up where people gather. Online and offline. Don't hide.
- Value – Offer something. Solve something. Even if it's small, do it well.
- Service – Be the answer to someone else's need, and watch how doors swing for you.

This is the real fulcrum of "Give, and it shall be given to you…"

Some of your greatest financial harvests won't come from heaven in a windstorm. They'll come from humans, disguised as divine partnerships, conversations, conflicts, and unexpected collaborations.

God hides money in men; not because He's tricky, but because He wants you to become humble enough to serve, wise enough to discern, and prepared enough to manage abundance when it comes.

Your channel to thriving value exchange is walking around in shoes. Say hello. Offer some help. Be ready to add value.

2nd Channel: Skills (Your Hands Has What Your Wallet Needs)

You can fast all you want, quote scriptures till your voice fades, sow seed on every altar in town, and dance like David danced. But until your hands begin to solve something, folks may clap, but your bank account won't. Skills are God's gift to your survival and prosperity on earth. Skills are the legs that carry your prayer requests to the bank. Skills are how God empowers you to feed nations without begging Pharaoh.

Many believers are sincere, but sincerely poor. And many poor people are sincerely idle, talent-wise. They are praying for miracles but ignoring methods. They are begging for breakthroughs while abandoning the tools in their own hands. But here's a truth that may sting: miracle money doesn't drop on lazy heads. It flows through skilled hands.

God blesses what you do, not what you intend to do. Ask the widow in 2 Kings 4: Elisha didn't ask her what she wanted. He asked her what she had in her house. She said "nothing... except a small jar of oil." That small jar was the skill, the value, the point of divine multiplication. God didn't pour oil from heaven. He used what her hand already carried. Your oil is your skill.

Skills are not just for professionals or craftsmen. Everyone has something they can develop, something they can sharpen, and something they can sell. Cooking is a skill. Teaching is a skill. Listening is a skill. Project management, singing, babysitting, sewing, speaking, editing, cleaning, building, digital design, any repeatable activity that solves a problem or creates delight can become a money channel if handled with excellence.

Some skills can be natural; like art, leadership, or public speaking. Some are acquired; like video editing, coding, or accounting. Both count. Both can feed you. But only if you're willing to cultivate them beyond comfort. The world does not pay you for what you enjoy. It pays you for what you can deliver consistently, excellently, and in demand.

You don't need to be the best. Just be visible, reliable, and better than you were last week. Let the improvement be measurable. Let your delivery be professional. And let your brand of excellence shine in whatever you do; even if it's selling roasted corn. People will pay a premium for consistent skill, anywhere, anytime.

Here's a rude awakening: the market does not respect your church attendance. It respects your competence. The Spirit of God can give you ideas, but He won't design the logo for you. He can nudge you toward YouTube, but He won't shoot your videos. He can whisper invention into your soul, but He won't code the app or write the pitch deck. That's your job. That's your skill zone. That's your money printer.

If you're still broke, ask yourself:

- What skills do I have that people need?
- What am I passionate about that I haven't turned into a service?
- What feedback have I received from others about something I do well?
- What can I learn in 30 days that could bring an additional income stream?
- What do I enjoy doing that could solve problems for others?

You may not do everything. But you can do something well enough to make it valuable. And if you think you have no skill, you're just untrained, not unskilled. Skill is not always talent. It is learned power. It is ability refined by repetition. Mastery is available to anyone who commits to practice and feedback.

Let's take it deeper: the level of financial flow you attract will almost always mirror the level of skill mastery you possess. Low skill, low pay. High skill, high pay. Specialized skill, rare pay. If you're not getting paid more, don't just blame the system. Refine your gift. Sharpen your edge. Go from casual to competent. Move from random to intentional. Extend from good to excellent.

You don't need 10 skills to prosper. You just need one skill expressed 10 different ways:

- One person writes. Another person teaches writing.
- One person cooks. Another person does cooking tutorials.
- One individual sings. Another individual coaches vocalists.
- One individual knows tech. Another individual trains tech teams.

Skill multiplies when expressed in different forms. Monetize your skill by applying it in services, courses, content, consultancy, and coaching. Package your knowledge. Document your process. Systemize your delivery.

And if you're spiritual, here's your advantage: you have access to divine intelligence. The Holy Spirit can give you insight on how to sharpen your skills faster, how to position them uniquely, and how to meet needs others can't see. That's not just skill, that's prophetic advantage.

But even with all the Holy Ghost downloads, God won't edit your videos for you. You must do the work.

Don't just pray for money. Sharpen your axe. Work your hands. Let your skills speak. Then your hands will begin to hold what your heart has been asking for.

3rd Channel: Problems (Every Crisis Carries a Cashflow)

Let's stop pretending. Money doesn't vanish. It relocates. Often, it relocates toward the person solving the most painful, urgent, or consistent problems. While many pray for wealth, the wise quietly position themselves at the junctions where pain and solution meet. And guess what? That junction is called Profit Street along the road to super-abundance.

Money doesn't always answer to prayer; it answers to problem-solving. That's why those who curse at problems often walk past prosperity. If you hate discomfort too much, you'll keep sidestepping the very doors that could lead you and your sown seed to abundance. Look carefully: every business you admire, every professional you celebrate, every solution you buy with your hard-earned cash, they're all just answers to someone's problem. Someone was hungry; KFC was born. Someone was bored; Netflix arrived. Someone needed to connect globally; Facebook showed up.

Problems birth platforms. Crises launch careers.

The difference between a broke man and a magnate is often this: one is running from problems but the other is running toward them.

You were not sent to Earth to avoid problems. You were sent to solve some. That's why your experience hurts in specific ways. That's why your heart burns at certain things which others ignore. That's why your background trained you in things others find confusing. God allows you to pass through a version of pain you are later anointed to solve for others. And in solving that version of pain, money follows.

Here's the hard truth: you will never really be free from problems. But you can choose to stop being the one with the problem and start being the one who solves it.

Solve problems, and money will look for you. Solve them faster, better, or cheaper than the next person, and wealth won't stop knocking on your door.

Ask Joseph. His journey to power was littered with problems: family betrayal, slavery, false accusation, imprisonment. Yet, it was Pharaoh's problem, a mysterious dream no one else could decode, that made room for Joseph in the palace. He interpreted the problem. He proposed a solution. He managed a crisis. That's value. That's money. That's promotion.

Dear believer, miracles don't just come from giving; they come from giving solutions. Jesus didn't just go around handing out gold coins. He healed. He taught. He raised the dead. He solved problems that systems couldn't. And multitudes followed Him, with their substance in hand.

Here's how to begin your own journey of profit through problems:

1. Observe the everyday pains people tolerate.

The best business ideas are often buried in complaints, inefficiencies, delays, or confusion. Listen for what annoys people. Eavesdrop on pain. Read product reviews. Look at what people wish were easier, better, faster, or cheaper. You don't need a billion-dollar problem. You just need one painful enough that people will pay to escape it.

2. Link the problem to your personality or passion.

Some problems will irritate you more than others. That's your clue. It may be because you're uniquely wired to solve it. Others hate the sight of blood; you're a nurse. Others avoid the sick; you feel called to care. Others hate chaos; you build systems. God usually wraps wealth inside a problem your heart refuses to ignore.

3. Design a simple solution first.

You don't need a perfect product. You need a workable start. An idea! A method! A message! A system! Start with version 1.0 and improve in due course. Perfection is a trap. Progress is your partner. Solve a small part of the problem now, and you can upgrade it later.

4. Communicate your solution clearly.

An excellent solution that nobody hears about will starve you. Learn how to share, show, and sell your solution. Use social media. Start a newsletter. Pitch to partners. Offer samples. Value that is seen becomes money that is sent.

5. Monetize creatively.

You can make money by solving problems through:

- Consulting
- Selling products
- Creating courses
- Offering services
- Licensing ideas
- Building communities

Even the most spiritual of men must learn to package their solution in forms others can pay for and benefit from: devotionals, podcasts, workbooks, eBooks, age-targeted solutions, downloadable apps, etc.

Here's a wake-up call: while you're sprinkling anointing oil, and quoting scriptures on wealth, someone out there is building an app that solves a problem for your entire neighbourhood; and they will get paid for it, whether they know Christ or not.

Why? Because money is blind to religion but drawn to results and solutions

Stop running from the hard questions. Start seeing yourself as a problem-solver-in-training. You're not just called to survive; you're called to carry divine intelligence that makes problems quake in your presence. You are an answer dressed as a human. It's time to stop just praying for money and start solving for it.

Problems are not obstacles. They are opportunities in work clothes. Behind every crisis is a currency. Behind every delay is a demand. Behind every pain is a payment.

Face the problems. Fix the problem. And watch financial flow follow your fingerprints.

4th Channel: Products and Services (Build What They Need, Earn What It's Worth)

Let's be honest: God won't do for you what He's empowered you to do for others. You're not going to "pray" your way into sustained financial flow if you don't have something of value you've wrapped into a product or service. And this right here is where many believers miss the bus. They love Jesus, but they offer nothing the marketplace can exchange for money.

Let this sink in: Money doesn't follow you because you're anointed. Money follows you because you offer something useful, consistent, and desirable in a package people can understand and pay for. That "something" is what we call a product or a service.

Every time you see money move, it's because someone gave value through a product or service, and someone else was willing to pay for it. Period! That's why God gave us brains, hands, creativity, and ideas, not just for worship, but for wealth creation through value provision.

Products and services are just value in a wrapper. They are the things you build, bake, fix, design, print, craft, write, deliver, or teach, to meet real needs, solve specific problems, or enhance someone's life.

Take a look around you. What do you eat? Someone sold it. What do you wear? Someone made it. What do you clean with, ride in, or scroll through on your phone? Products and services. If you don't have one in the game, you're simply a player in the gallery. It's time to get on the field.

The Rule Is Simple: If you want money consistently, create value repeatedly. If you want more money, solve deeper problems or serve more people.

The Bible says in Proverbs 11:26,

> "The people will curse him who withholds grain, but blessing will be on the head of him who sells it." (NKJV)

Did you see that? Not just the one who gives it away, but the one who sells it! Blessings are on those who put their value on display and release it for exchange. That's divine economics.

So how do you start?

1. Identify what you're already doing for free.

What are people always asking you for help with? Advice? Design? Prayer? Strategy? Makeup? Writing? Ideas? Cakes? Repairs? That may be your raw material. You've probably served your first ten clients for free without even knowing. But now it's time to build it into a sellable form.

2. Package your value.

Make it tangible. Make it clear. Make it buyable. Turn your knowledge into a course. Turn your skills into a coaching service. Turn your hobby into a product line. Turn your expertise into templates, guides, books, or systems. Whatever is invisible must become visible and transferable. That's the difference between a dreamer and an entrepreneur.

3. Test it. Prove it. Improve it.

Don't wait for perfection. Launch something simple. Serve your first three paying clients. Let them use your product. Gather feedback. Polish your process. Products evolve, and services get sharper with use. The market is your teacher. Don't despise the days of small, clumsy beginnings.

4. Price it with conviction.

Stop apologizing for charging. Jesus said, "The labourer is worthy of his wages." You are not begging for money; you are exchanging value for value. Set a fair price. Add profit. And don't be afraid to adjust upward when you level up. Cheap is not holy. Free is not always wise.

5. Promote it consistently.

If they don't see it, they can't buy it. Visibility is part of your responsibility. Learn how to market. Talk about what you offer. Show results. Tell stories. Share testimonials. Offer samples. Ask for referrals. Remember, even Jesus didn't hide His service. He said, "Go and tell what you have seen and heard."

6. Diversify when stable.

Once your product or service has gained traction, build related offers. Serve more needs within your niche. Offer premium versions. Upsell. Bundle. License. Collaborate. Expand your capacity. Add a digital layer. The deeper your value-exchange tree, the broader your income branches.

God never told you to "just be there." He gave you hand to create and a mind to multiply. And if you look through the parable of the talents, one thing is clear: those who hid what they were given were called wicked. Those who used what they were given were called faithful; and they were given more.

Products and services are divine permission to participate in God's wealth strategy. He gives you seed, you must sow it into the soil of value, build a product or offer a service, and multiply it. Waiting for miracle money without value in hand is not faith. It is wishful thinking.

You don't need to beg to be blessed. You need to build something that blesses others consistently and watch how heaven partners with your obedience, innovation, and diligence. When value flows out from you, income flows in to you.

5th Channel: Ideas (Invisible Assets That Print Visible Riches)

The world runs on ideas. Your breakthrough, your business, your brand, your wealth, they're all disguised as ideas. But here's the painful twist: ideas don't look like money. That's why most people ignore them. They only see the seed, not the tree. They want fruit, not roots. They want harvest, not process. But money is an echo, not a source. It is the reward of a worked-out idea.

God gives seed to the sower, and many times, that seed is consumed, or separated at best, only to be eaten later. But that unassuming, unimpressive, inconvenient seed is potent enough to be mixed with an idea, a burden, a thought, a solution, a wild imagination, an irritating nudge. If you ignore your idea, you sabotage your stream. Ideas are currency in disguise, and the Holy Spirit often whispers wealth not through bank alerts, but through mental downloads.

Remember Joseph in Egypt? God didn't rain down cash on Pharaoh. He sent an idea through a dream; and Joseph had the divine intelligence to interpret and execute it. The famine didn't kill them because an idea was honoured. In every generation, God releases treasures through thoughts. Only the discerning and diligent can decode them.

So how do you turn ideas into income?

1. Capture Everything.

Stop trusting your brain to remember brilliance. Write it. Record it. Sketch it. Ideas are like vapour. They vanish if not captured. Your phone is not just for Instagram; use its notes app. Use voice memos. Have a notebook in your bag. Some of your million-dollar doors are already floating around your head; waiting to be pinned down.

You don't know which idea is your Joseph moment. Some will be raw. Some might be ugly. Others will make no sense at first. That's fine. God doesn't drop diamonds, He drops stones, and waits to see who will polish them.

2. Test and Trim.

Every idea is not urgent. Every idea is not viable. Some are divine, others are distractions. Test them. Bounce them off trusted voices. Research your market. Look for evidence. Does this solve a real problem? Will people pay for it? Can you build it? Will it scale?

Don't get emotionally married to every "revelation." Some are to be parked. Some are to be passed. Others are to be pursued now. Wisdom is knowing what to do with what you've received.

3. Work it into a System.

Ideas don't pay until they're converted into systems, structures, and solutions. The idea of Uber became a multi-billion-dollar app. The idea of Airbnb became a global empire. The idea of TOMS became a social impact machine. The idea of Netflix disrupted an entire industry. But without structure, they would have stayed as exciting dreams and motivational tweets.

Your idea must become a framework: a product, a service, a platform, a brand, a blueprint, a movement. You must go beyond the brilliance of the moment and enter the grind of building it out. That's where money lives.

4. Protect and Position.

If your idea is original, protect it. File that IP. Trademark that phrase. Document that process. Your idea is spiritual property with physical implications. Don't let mediocrity steal what God planted in you through carelessness.

Then, position it. Get it in front of the right people. Share it with clarity. Brand it well. Package it with excellence. An idea may be anointed, but if it looks like confusion or feels like chaos, the market will reject it.

Position is not pride. Presentation is not vanity. They are both wisdom strategies that increase credibility and invite compensation.

5. Monetize With Integrity.

Ideas are meant to serve. But service doesn't mean free. If your idea saves time, solves problems, enhances lives, or changes outcomes, you deserve to be paid. Create income channels around it. License it. Teach it. Sell it. Offer consulting. Publish it. Build tools. Launch a brand. Build a subscription. Form a company.

But keep your heart clean. Don't exploit people's pain. Don't over-promise and under-deliver. God will never back you if you manipulate others in His name. Build wealth with truth, value, and excellence.

The devil doesn't fear a Christian who shouts, "I receive!" He fears the one who hears, builds, refines, and launches an idea that solves problems with integrity and power. That's why hell fights your mind, because it knows your next level is not locked in your bank account; it's buried in your head.

You may not have rich parents, a powerful network, or a large inheritance. But if you will steward the idea factory in your spirit, and work it until it becomes wealth on earth, you will not die average. Many people are praying for miracle money. But those who partner with God in birthing and deploying ideas will attract money daily, because money serves those who serve humanity with value.

You are one God-breathed idea away from changing your financial story forever.

But don't just think it. Don't just talk it. Build it.

6th Channel: Systems (Where Your Seed Learns to Multiply Without You)

There are channels that require sweat. Others, sense. But systems? They require submission. Not to fate, but to principles. Not to hype, but to patterns. Wealthy people don't hustle harder than you; they plug in smarter than you. While many are chasing quick money in dusty corners and volatile ventures, the wise are quietly growing generational wealth in established systems. They don't only work for money. They make money work in a system, and that system multiplies it while they sleep.

Let's settle it: money doesn't grow because you pray hard. It grows because you plant it in fertile, proven systems that have built-in mechanisms for growth: systems like dividend-paying stocks, bonds, treasury bills, automated crypto bots, savings schemes, real estate REITs, and well-managed ETFs. These aren't buzzwords for Wall Street elites. These are proven gates. And those who find them early enough walk out of labour into leverage.

Systems are silent multipliers. They don't need to make noise to yield results. They don't beg for attention. They're like quiet engines running beneath a floor. If you plug in right, they carry you faster than effort alone ever could. But if you ignore them, you'll keep doing in 10 years what others finish in 2, because they trusted what you were too distracted to study.

Let's demystify it.

The stock market isn't a playground for greedy traders. It's a platform where real businesses share their profits with those wise enough to own a slice of its future. When you own shares in a thriving company, your money is working in its system, while you focus on building yours. A bond is not a magical instrument. It's just your money earning interest from a government or corporation in due course, safely. What about Treasury bills? That's your money doing federal work for you, not on the street, but in the spreadsheets of nations.

Every day, your ignorance is making someone else rich. When you ignore the power of automated investing, someone else uses that system to collect dividends. When you keep your money in a bank savings account with less than 1% yield, someone else has their money riding on a compound-interest rocket. It's not about greed. It's about stewardship. God doesn't multiply what you store; He multiplies what you sow, and systems are a kind of soil.

The wealthy have long known that systems compound advantage. While others sleep with anxiety, their money is wide awake: trading metals, monitoring indexes, adjusting to inflation, sniffing market signals, making calculated micro-decisions. That's not magic. That's automation. You don't need to be a market genius. You need to trust and learn a system.

Yes, systems require risk. But the biggest risk is ignorance. A system can be understood. It can be tested. It can be simulated and tracked. It can be optimized. Unlike blind hustle, systems come with data. And data is like a prophet: it tells you what's coming before it comes. God gave you a brain, not just a prayer tongue. And heaven blesses the builder who studies blueprints before laying bricks.

Do you want to unearth wealth through systems?

- Study index funds that grow with the global economy.
- Look into Robo advisors that balance your portfolio based on your risk appetite.
- Explore real estate income trusts (REITs) that let you earn rent without owning a building.
- Learn about peer-to-peer lending, forex auto-trade bots, and long-term crypto staking protocols that reward consistency over hype.
- Find dividend aristocrats, stocks that have paid growing dividends for over 25 years.

All of these are vehicles. But the destination is financial independence. Not so you can boast, but so you can breathe. So you can serve without begging, give without guilt, bless without breaking, and live beyond just surviving.

One system may not make you rich overnight. But multiple systems, with discipline, time, and informed decisions, will take you farther than emotional giving or reckless spending ever could. Some systems offer 4–5% returns yearly. Some offer 15–20% with higher risk. Others, like automated commodity trading or crypto bots, may yield higher returns with a learning curve. But here's the rule: invest only in what you understand or can be taught to understand. Systems reward students, not gamblers.

So what do you do now?

Start where you are. Learn what you can. Begin with safe systems. Use simulators. Open a practice investment account. Read one finance newsletter daily. Speak with certified advisors, not street prophets. And in due course, build a hybrid wealth engine, where your skills bring in income, but your systems compound wealth.

Let others run the rat race. You? Build tunnels. Lay pipes. Set systems. That's what kings do. They don't chase riches. They build flows.

There is no substitute for Your Seed

When the word of God says in Genesis chapter 1 and verse 29, **I have given you**..., then I ask: *Where is your own herb-bearing or tree yielding* seed? *What did you do with yours? What are you doing with yours?*

Why are you eating your herb-bearing and tree-yielding seeds? Understand this: whatever you eat has reached the end of its voyage, no matter the substances and capabilities of its content. Its only remaining destination is the latrine. You would have noticed that your poo looks almost the same, whether you eat bread or seed? That same mistake, eating seed with bread, is possibly why poverty looks so similar everywhere you go, whether among Africans, Latinos, or mixed races.

Why did you hand over your seed to your pastor? Aren't you being just a little naïve? Prayer is never a substitute for the seed you are expected to sow in your field. Laying on of hands will not reproduce your herb-bearing or tree-yielding seed. Shouting the loudest hallelujah will never resurrect seed that's already been consumed. Give offering, pay tithes, but remember: your seed is meant for a field of endeavour, a business, an investment, or human capacity building, where it can multiply and return with a harvest.

Many times, the pastor you give your seed to is busy sowing it into ventures and investments that are already yielding bread, seed, and fruit for him and his family. This does not undermine the genuine efforts and single-mindedness of some church leaders whose pursuit centers on missions, evangelism, and discipleship. It also does not invalidate the vision and strategies of pastors who pursue God-given mandates beyond the exclusive walls of Christian ministry. Both approaches are strategic and relevant.

But remember this: whenever you hear a pastor saying, "I can never be poor again," it is usually because he has learned and practiced the same principles that many Christian folks prayerfully overlook. While you are innocently giving *'breakthrough offering'* and *'painful sacrifices'* waiting for heaven to split open, some pastors are building printing presses, media companies, advertising agencies, schools, real estate portfolios, and investing in profitable businesses. When you naively give away your own miracle-filled, herb bearing, and tree yielding seeds with your 'fervent' prayers, are you still wondering why your own miracle hasn't arrived? What more do you expect God to help you with? God cannot be mocked. Whatever you sow in your own field is what you will reap.

Should a pastor invest? Of course, if it aligns with his vision and purpose. No pastor is exempt from the unchanging principles of Scripture. And as for the church member, you are simply inexcusable.

Where is the venture into which you sowed your herb-bearing seed? Where is the field of investment into which you planted your tree-yielding seed? Do you know anyone, dead or alive, who became truly wealthy by salary alone? God is just. He never stops giving you your portion. And you too are without excuse because you receive your portion regularly. Either you separate and sow your seed, and journey further on the road to riches, or you eat it all as bread and watch yourself slip further on the way to penury. Whatever you do with your seed is the determining factor of your eventual outcome.

Whichever voyage you choose for your seed brings results to your life equivalent to the choices and actions you make along those paths. Strangely, a man's seed is so magnetic that it inevitably drags along the seedlord himself on that same journey, either along the road to penury or the byway to superabundance.

Chapter 12

Roaming the Crowded Lane to Poverty

The heavens bear witness to the express permission given by those who roam the pathway to poverty, for their provisions to be confined to the layer of basic supply, regardless of how glamorous their lives may appear on the surface. Along this route, the ground on which to stand is shaky, the field of true value is deserted, and the harvest is deservedly commensurate. God is ever just and never withholds harvest from sown seed. He multiplies to everyone the harvest of whatever seed is planted. But wherever people are at ease to sow nothing and untroubled to reap nothing, today may mask their dormant chain with layers upon layers of makeup, but time is guaranteed to reveal the drought behind their disguise.

Poverty doesn't sneak in; it marches boldly down the path we often pave ourselves, one squandered seed at a time. It is ready to pounce and ready to ensnare countless voyagers in its suffocating grip. Once it seizes control of your seed, it shows no mercy to your toddlers and no respect for your pregnant woman. In its unforgiving clutches, there is no reverence for your rank or post, no deference to your privilege or pedigree. Its grip is ruthless, untouched by your dreams, unbothered by your title, be it graduate or general. Once in control, it's totally resolute to finish up the seed meant for tomorrow's triumphs. The moment you agree to tread its established pathway, its force knows no boundaries, recognizes no distinctions, and spares no one from its insidious grasp. As long as you remain within its territory, consuming your seed month by month, it cares not for the color of your skin, the dialect on your lips, or the faith in your heart.

Whether you live in the bustling metropolises of the developed world or the remote villages of the global south, the pathway to poverty is paved with tokens of the same raw mix. They are woven with concretes of a similar formula, coated with comparable sealants all around. Its reinforcement is rock-solid against any sudden breakaway, and once you sign up, even unknowingly, it collects your subscription, monthly, mercilessly. Give it its due and watch how it ravages with blights and erodes the foundations of hope and dignity with ruthless efficiency. As long as you are treading this path with its regular subscription, consuming your seed, wasting your seasons, there can be no illusions of immunity or invincibility, even if your passage is through sheer ignorance or by express permission.

Guess what materials are used to pave the pathway to poverty anywhere across the globe: poor decisions, wasteful habits, the wrong focus for income generation, and a mindset that confuses consumption for success.

1. Voyagers' Consume-it-all Mindset

The shadow of poverty looms large along this pathway, casting its dark pall over the lives of billions of voyagers who are recipients of its brutal force. Yet, behind the tangible hardship and durable deprivation lies a more insidious force exerted on all travelers–the consumption mindset. It is an inescapable state of mind that traps individuals in a web of consume-it-all lifestyles and self-limiting beliefs. It is a cycle of poverty that never lets go of its victims. From generation to generation, this invisible shackle tightens its grip around the necks of those traveling this route, condemning them to a fate of present struggles and future stagnation. If there is any room for a moment of holiday midway, it's all about "not enough"

This lane promotes a viewpoint of scarcity–a pervasive sense of insufficiency that infiltrates every aspect of life as though it is impossible to find any seed in a voyager's meager income. It manifests its philosophy through flawed financial habits, like unbridled consumption, zero savings, under-saving, and diversion of savings from one month to another. It propagates its creed through limiting behaviors characterized by financial recklessness, zero value creation or addition, and so perpetuates a cycle of shortage, not-enough, and false hope that entraps all travelers along this vicious road. Meanwhile, someone other than themselves or something untoward is usually to blame –parents, background, employer, government, spirits, or inherited curses–for their state of never-enough.

At its core, the consume-it-all mindset is characterized by a sense of resignation and mental limitation—a belief that one's circumstances are fixed and irreversible, and that an escape from the throes of too little is an unattainable dream. Born out of self-doubt and reinforced by false hope, this mindset breeds the hope of some abrupt future financial miracles in those it ensnares, even when they willingly refuse the proven system that leads there.

The influence of this type of mindset extends beyond the realm of an individual road user. It reverberates through the collective consciousness of all voyagers along the way. Just as a single drop creates ripples that spread across the surface of a pond, the collective mindset along this route shapes their culture, values, and aspirations. The surroundings are rife with financial illiteracy, something-to-consume, someone-to-blame, and never-enough-to-keep-a-seed syndrome; all of which stem from the same poverty mindset. Any potential to escape the rat race becomes stifled by the range of their individual mentality, aided by the weight of their collective conviction.

The impact of this kind of mindset is widespread. Individuals who adopt the consume-it-all philosophy will normally shy away from pursuing supplementary undertakings to increase their earning potential. They can pile up dozens of arguments against the pursuit of enterprise because they are too convinced of its inevitable failure, anyway. Fearful of failure and unwilling to take risks, they easily resign themselves to a life of wage-only labor and economic deficiency, sometimes working more than one shift but consuming whatever they get to earn, every month, every year. This wicked mindset perpetuates the cycle of poverty for voyagers on this path and, most times, prepares the way for their future generation in economic, mental, and emotional terms.

The journey itself exerts a profound influence on their own economic, mental, and emotional balance, aggravating the toll of scarcity with the burden of distress. Chronic stress, worry, and depression are all too common among voyagers here, as the relentless pressure of debt, financial insecurity, and social relegation takes its toll on mental health. In fact, the stigma and shame associated with the level of poverty along this route further isolate individuals and compound their feelings of despair and defeatism.

In the absence of saved and sown seed, the poverty mindset becomes a self-reinforcing cycle, as voyagers soon begin to internalize their circumstances as evidence of some inherited spells, or lack of luck, or some other external influences meddling in their affairs. Lacking access to correct scriptural wisdom, selfless mentors, and opportunities for personal growth, they remain trapped in a state of learned helplessness, resign to the belief that their fate is beyond their control, and start looking for some get-rich-quick shortcuts and money-miracles from 'money doublers'–some within and some others outside the church.

2. Voyagers' Wrong Focus for Income Generation

One of the most crucial elements noticeable along the pathway to poverty is that practically all travellers, wherever located under heaven, are preoccupied with the same set of misleading and off-target channels for income generation. This is a limiting challenge, because the objects of their focus neither multiply seeds nor amplify fruits. Rather, the channels on which they concentrate either help deplete their income much quicker or keep it at the same level even when the proceeds get raised.

Those who travel this route completely focus on such income channels that can only support addition over a long period, but can never attract multiplication or attain exponential dimensions because of the limitations of their focus.

Income generation channels for travelers along this route are in three categories:

- Remuneration-based Channels
- Luck-Based Channels.
- Less-for-More Channels.

A. Remuneration-Based Channels: These are channels that offer fixed or variable (same or comparable) regular compensation in income for at least 2 consecutive seasons, often negotiated and determined in advance.

Common Features of Remuneration-Based Channels

- Any increment is based on what your sweat, skills, or time alone can offer.
- Any increment comes in trickles of addition, extras, and add-ons.
- Any sustainable increment comes perhaps after 2 or more consecutive seasons.
- Earners' unavailability suspends or totally stops income and add-ons

Key examples:

i. Salary: Fixed regular payment given on a monthly basis to an employee for their work or services rendered to an organization.
ii. Hourly wages: Payments based on the number of hours worked.
iii. Small business: A privately owned enterprise with a relatively low volume of sales and a handful of employees.
iv. Freelance income: Earnings from self-employment or contracting work.
v. Commission: Income based on sales or transactions.
vi. Tips and gratuities: Additional payments received in service-based industries.
vii. Bonuses and overtime pay: Additional compensation based on achievements or extra performance.

viii. Pension or retirement income: Regular payments received after retiring from employment.

ix. Borrowing for consumption: A pattern of behavior where individuals excessively rely on borrowing, such as taking out loans or using credit cards, to fund their consumption habits and maintain a certain lifestyle beyond their means.

B. **Luck-Based Channels**: These are channels primarily dependent on chance or random events rather than individual efforts or skills. Despite the very rare occurrence of luck-based wins, many travelers queue behind these channels day after day. When did you last find money on the ground? How many people do you know who became rich through finding money or lucky draws? There is a high chance of one in a million people, but hopefuls stay glued to these channels, which seldom bring in any sustainable income to luck-seekers, no matter what efforts they put in.

Common Features of Luck-based Channels

- It is unpredictable and requires no serious planning or effort from the recipient.
- It relies heavily on chance or random events rather than individual effort, skill, or merit.
- Income varies greatly, ranging from small handouts, often less than what is invested (a very common outcome), to significant sums of money (which is extremely rare).

- It is unreliable for consistent earnings since it is not under the control of the individual receiving it.
- There is no guarantee of success or profit, but the chances of loss are very high.

Key Examples include:

i. Lottery winnings: Money expected to be won through lottery games, where the outcome is based purely on chance.
ii. Gambling winnings: Income expected from games of chance, such as casinos, poker, or sports betting.
iii. Contest prizes: Monetary prizes or rewards through contests, sweepstakes, or competitions.
iv. Inheritance: Waiting to be rich through money or assets expected from the estate of a relative or benefactor.
v. Unexpected windfalls: Hoping for unexpected sizeable sums of money through gifts, bonuses, or unexpected financial gains.
vi. Found fortune: Hoping to discover money or valuable items unexpectedly, such as winning a treasure hunt, or finding lost gold or items with significant value while diving, digging, or performing random activities.

C. **Less-for-More Channels**: These are channels that promise more-for-less but take away far more than they give out.

Common Features of Less-for-More Channels

- These channels are associated with a lack of patience and willingness to endure the gradual process of wealth accumulation through consistent saving, investing, and prudent financial management.
- Focus is on immediate gratification and consumption, often at the expense of long-term financial planning, stability, or savings goals.
- There is an overemphasis on quick and effortless wealth accumulation.
- There is a high tolerance of risk and a blatant willingness to gamble with finances in pursuit of quick profits.
- The pursuit of quick wealth makes voyagers more susceptible to scams, fraud, and deceptive financial schemes, promising unrealistic returns.

Key examples
- Get rich quick: This is a mindset or belief that one can quickly and easily accumulate wealth with no careful planning, hard work, or patience. Thus, individuals often hunt for shortcuts or

schemes promising rapid financial success, often overlooking the risks and potential consequences involved.

- Money-doubling Schemes: Typically refer to schemes or fraudulent activities that prey on individuals seeking quick and easy ways to increase their wealth. Such schemes come with promises that investors' money would be doubled or multiplied within a short period, often through investment opportunities or financial transactions. "

3. Voyagers eat their seeds, leaving their success to luck and destiny

Along this road, many travelers share the practice of eating their seed with bread, then searching for financial miracles from other places. Whereas, God graciously keeps financial miracles within the seed– with multiplication and exponential powers, and commits to actualizing these powers when those seeds are sown, yet voyagers eat their seed and then resort to seeking financial miracles from prayers, hope, and some commitments to church activities. Hope is good, prayer works tremendous powers, and your church commitment is commendable, but none of those is a scriptural management strategy for financial prosperity, as is erroneously believed and wrongly adopted by travelers along the path to poverty.

1. <u>Voyagers see seed and bread as the same</u>: Voyagers do not see any distinction between seed and bread, and so never separate their seed from their bread. Rather, they consume all! They never see the seed as the essence of continuity, the lifeblood of tomorrow's harvest, and the very soul of wealth creation. In a moment of dire short-sightedness, they follow the same tragic narrative of all past and present voyagers on the pathway to poverty, devouring their seed alongside their bread.

According to the principles of God's provision, every income earner is expected to stand as a steward of the harvest, entrusted with the sacred duty of sowing the seeds of today's provision for tomorrow's bounty. Your seeds are not merely raw materials for food but phenomenal crucibles of life, wherein lies God's full-capacity engine pre-programmed with encrypted instructions and systems to give birth to its kind in multiplication and exponential powers. Yet, along this vicious road lies a perilous temptation—the allure of immediate gratification at the cost of future abundance. It is this extreme allure that drives ignorant and reckless voyagers to the throes of desperation and reckless abandon and coerces them to succumb to the seductive whispers of instant indulgence.

2. <u>Voyagers carelessly manage any forced seed.</u> In a scramble to break free from the shackles of poverty, some voyagers half-heartedly separate their seed from bread, but keep it carelessly. Some others

reluctantly separate seed from their bread but invest it carelessly, because they are too mentally lazy to research any acclaimed investment before putting in their hard-earned and hard-separated seed. A larger percentage of the very few voyagers who separate and sow their seeds along this route do not have the necessary and sufficient knowledge of the chosen field, venture, or investment before sowing therein.

How tragic it is to work hard and earn, exercise such uncommon restraint in order to separate your seed, only to pour it into an unknown investment just because an uncle (who is also in the same sinking boat) said it is an excellent investment? Such is the norm along this route. Voyagers here seldom sow, but when they do so, it is done recklessly on barren fields, because of their ignorance of or refusal to conform to the immutable laws of sowing and harvest. They forsake the principles between the layers of basic supplies and multiplication, severing the very thread of continuity by sowing on barren fields that an equally ignorant relative or co-worker hurriedly introduced to them.

The consequences of such folly are as predictable as they are catastrophic. Their storehouses lack seeds of renewal, their patched fields lie fallow, and their promised lush and flourishing investment turns barren and becomes a wasteland without remedy. What was expected to be brimming with abundance will then echo hollowly, mocking their expectation with its silent emptiness. Hunger then gnaws at their bellies, and despair weighs heavily upon their souls as they confront the bitter harvest of their own ill-informed short-sightedness. Many then run to the church and pastors for sudden miracles.

And soon after a year or two of hard labor, they gather seeds from far and wide only to pour the same into similar, unknown investments again!

3. <u>Voyagers earn more to consume more</u>: Voyagers sometimes see the need to spend money to increase their personal capacity to get better at whatever they do, especially when it is presented as an avenue to earn more. But when they increase personal capacity and earn more, they consume all additional income on frivolities. Promotion, bonus, or higher pay at the workplace receives an immediate and commensurate response with newer gadgets, exclusive subscriptions, and a more expensive apartment in a more expensive part of town.

Voyagers here sometimes appear comfortable before their neighbors but are in reality over-stressed and over-stretched from the clutches of debt and discretionary consumption, which combine efforts to gnaw their souls. They wait in hope for a better job and higher pay that will someday solve all their money problems while they remain loyal to this distressing pathway and its overarching lifestyle.

4. <u>No budgeting, no planning</u>: An otherwise promising life gets left to destiny and chance on this route. Loan is their ally, credit cards are their motivation, and discretionary spending is their travel companion. Without taking care of today, they believe that tomorrow will take care of itself. Voyagers eat the seed of today's multiplication with yesterday's debt and are warming up to pay today's debt with the seed of tomorrow's increase. Their only source of income is their salary; their only hope of meeting those growing expenses (loan and interest repayment, kids' school fees, rent, subscriptions, vehicle maintenance, feeding, transportation) is their next paycheck. Salary comes in one way, goes out in seven different ways, and leaves three other ways till next month's paycheck. Their stimulus is their false sense of security–job security. Their advisers are people on the same road, heading in the same direction. As the economy nosedives, their expenses increase; and their liabilities become more formidable. Yet, there is no planning, there is no discretion. There is no room for self-denial unless their money is insufficient for instant indulgence and the seller is unprepared to sell on credit.

Occasionally, when accidentally coaxed into investing in a field or operating a venture, they apply their life's philosophy to their venture and investment without thorough planning and adequate preparation–

leaving all to chance and destiny. They don't put in place proper checks and balances before rushing in, and they don't consider systems and controls in order to safeguard their accidental vineyard, venture, or investment.

In the end, luck proves itself an unreliable and unscriptural management strategy for life. Destiny proves itself, time and time again, that it is a terrible manager of business and investment, except that voyagers on the pathway to poverty never learn the lessons.

5. Many Voyagers Hope to Kick-start Investment with Future Gratuity: A seed in the ground needs seasons to grow; not a rush in the end, not a last-minute show, but many voyagers prefer to wait till retirement before planting seeds from (or with) their gratuity. They are calculative because of the expected bulk pay. They therefore want to be penny-wise when they have been pound-foolish for decades. Though this is like planting seeds in winter's snow, it's oddly the only satisfying and straightforward choice for many trapped and far along on the highway to penury.

A decade of growth beats a late, hurried dash, but not in the appraisal of those who travel this route. What wisdom is there in waiting so long, when compounding always, unavoidably, follows through with its mandatory wealth-building tenure? This is tragically the thinking cap of many full-fledged voyagers en route to their destination hand-to-mouth, aiming to delay the planting of their seeds till when they no longer have anywhere to hide, when they cannot readily scramble or unscramble, when they no longer hold the power to weather the tide.

Time and patience are two dominant factors necessary to compound your seed, but at retirement, you don't have the luxury of time; you don't have the indulgence of patience. Time transforms modest monthly investments into a golden opportunity through the extraordinary power of compound interest. But each year a voyager spends waiting is a precious seed unplanted, and a potential forest of wealth left ungrown. Wisdom teaches us that sustainable abundance comes from consistent, patient efforts. Those who postpone investing until their farewell party miss the melody of growth that patience plays out over decades. Those who delay leave their stories untold and their forest of wealth unsown.

Gratuity, though valuable, was never meant to be your first investment–rather, it should be the crowning jewel in a well-tended garden of financial growth. When retirement looms, it's not the best time to start planting; it's the season to harvest what should have been growing all along, but disoriented voyagers will not borrow wisdom. They would rather ask the solitary vessel of their gratuity to shoulder their entire remaining investment journey, akin to expecting a gentle breeze to power an ocean crossing.

At the end, it's usually a very bitter retirement regret to realize that time, a most valuable asset in compounding, has slipped away unenlisted; and patience, a most precious ally that powers growing riches, cannot do a thorough work, cannot complete its full cycle.

Chapter 13

Switching Lane to Wealth Creation Bypass

Only a few transformations are as profound or as consequential as the transition from the *Fast-Lane-to-Poverty* to *Prosperity Bypass*. The path to poverty is paved with a state of consciousness. It is characterized by a pervasive sense of lack, not just material, but mental, and governed by a mindset allergic to possibility. It is a well-worn track where multitudes march unknowingly, prisoners of invisible chains, limitation, fear, and cycles dressed as tradition. But the Prosperity Bypass? Ah, it is carved by covenant. It is paved not with hustle, but with clarity of intention. It begins when you believe, violently and audaciously, that God did not place you on earth to barely survive. That you were wired to create value, shape reality, and walk as an agent of divine abundance. Grounded in the principles of value creation and value addition, this route liberates individuals from the shackles of limitation and not-enough, empowering them to attract and cultivate wealth with clarity, intention, and abundance.

This is no casual stroll. It is a deeply personal and transformative odyssey; one that unfolds on multiple levels: mental, emotional, spiritual, and financial. It demands war against inherited poverty codes, a dismantling of every altar where "not enough" was worshipped as virtue. You must confront the inner saboteur, silence the echo of scarcity, and surrender to a vision bigger than your upbringing. This path will not let you remain the same. It will stretch your standards. It will offend your old comfort zone. And it will crown you, if you endure, with the kind of wealth that doesn't rot, doesn't rule you, and doesn't steal your soul. This is not just a route change; it is a renaissance. It is a far-reaching transition that requires you to welcome some deviations from many previous norms and adopt a new set of standards altogether. And those who take it don't just prosper; they prophesy prosperity by how they live.

The transition is easier and takes a shorter road for those at the ***Barely Enough*** level of poverty because, though they are trapped, they are trapped with tools in their hands. They already sit near the gates of wealth, but doubt, habits, and the comfort of status hold them back. A few disciplined turns toward Value Creation, a ruthless honoring of Seed & Bread, and a faithful practice of Seedtime & Harvest can flip their story in months. The ***Hardly Enough*** have more leaks in their financial roof because their climb is steeper, but with focused obedience to the same laws, they too can emerge, though their journey demands greater sacrifice and grit.

For those trapped at the level of ***Alleviated Poverty***, the climb is not just uphill; it begins from another man's shoulders. Progress requires breaking free from dependence before even touching productivity. And for those imprisoned by ***Aggravated Poverty***, the journey is a fight for breath before it becomes a fight for bread. And if you can see the seed that carries heaven's algorithm lumped together with your bread early enough, you can grow your roots sturdy enough to overrun any of your walls. The path may be longer, the cost may be heavier, the climb may be steeper, but the destination is the same if you follow the laws of *Value Creation*, **Seed & Bread**, and **Seedtime & Harvest** in that order. Those laws do not lie. Value Creation births income, Seed & Bread preserves the future, and Seedtime & Harvest multiplies it. Obey the sequence, and even the most desolate soil can grow a harvest.

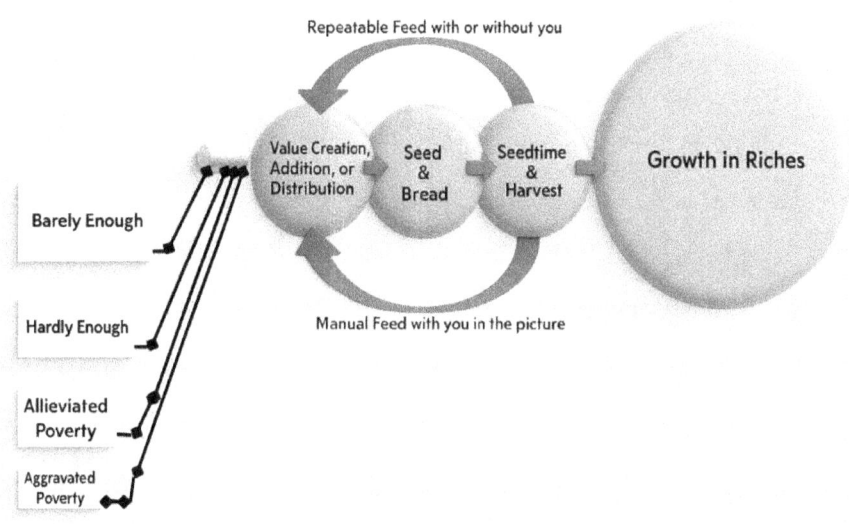

You can exit poverty from where you are

This route is not a tourist trail. It is a sacred refinement ground. Every step burns away the excess, every mile demands the core. It is marked by drive, truth, and a radical reimagining of who you were born to be.

- Self-examination: This route will drag you into the mirror and demand that you see, not your filters, not your fears, but the raw roots of poverty's grip. It will demand scrutinizing those inherited mindsets, whispered lies, and generational echoes that chant "not enough." You must interrogate your beliefs like a prophet confronting idols. Until you name the patterns, they will keep you bound. And unless you expose the rot in your thinking, the seed of abundance cannot germinate. This isn't self-help. It's self-surgery.
- Perspective Shift: There will come a divinely orchestrated point where your beliefs will buckle. And they must because no man walks into kingdom abundance while still bowing at the altar of limitation. You will question your theology of lack. You will smash the mirror of victimhood. And then, like a warrior-priest, you will rise with fresh eyes, eyes that see yourself not as a statistic, but as a strategist; not as a victim, but a vessel of divine prosperity. You will come to see yourself, not as a bystander to fate, but as a co-architect in the unfolding of divine intention, as a co-creator of the outcome of your own purpose.
- Inspired Action: This path is not paved with passive prayers. It demands inspired action, drenched in a deep sense of purpose and passion. It demands action, not from panic or performance, but from divine clarity, as the catalyst for transformation and the bridge that connects your dreams to your reality. Every step must answer a holy call: to build, to learn, to rise, to risk. Whether it is seeking education and training, sharpening your craft, launching a

value-driven venture, or daring to pitch in rooms they said you don't belong, you move, because God said move. This is how dreams stop floating and start forming.

➢ Fire-Tested Resilience: You will be resisted. Hell will not applaud your exit from poverty. Life will throw delays, discouragements, and detours. But here lies the mystery: your scars are the soil of your strength. Every failure is fertilizer, and every setback, a sharpening. This is not mere perseverance; it is covenantal stubbornness. It is a refusal to die in the desert when you were destined for Canaan. And as you press through the fire, what emerges is not just a survivor, but a steward of glory. One who has been refined by pressure and preserved by purpose.

Welcome to a transformative voyage.

1st Interchange:

Special-Purpose Road Signs: Change Your Mindset

The mindset with which you approach value-creation and addition holds the key to the attainment and sustenance of riches. On this road, your mind emerges as the weaver of your reality, shaping your world through the lens of dream and belief. Before kingdom riches ever appear in your hand, value must first be formed in your head. Before you touch multiplication in your bank account, you must conquer limitations in your belief system. From the smallest units of everyday value-addition to the grandest dreams of turning your seed into building blocks of global products and services, your mindset serves as the compass guiding your journey, influencing every thought, action, and interaction. The mindset empowers you to wisely separate, properly cultivate, and carefully sow your seed with clarity, intention, and direction.

You want kingdom riches, real riches, not the crumbs of survival, but the kind that echoes through generations? Then understand this: Every fortune ever built in the kingdom began as a single thought. That single thought metamorphosed into a product or service, which transformed into money, and the money grew into riches. The right mindset mobilizes heaven in your direction. It separates you from the crowd of consumers and calls you into the covenant of creators. It helps you name your field, define your offering, shape your products, and steward your ideas with prophetic clarity and generational precision.

The transformative power of mindset is quite manifest on this road, where individuals possess the ability to inspire, influence, and mobilize themselves toward a value-based offering. The mindset is the foundation upon which your field of investment or business unit is built. Like a sculptor shaping clay, your mind shapes the course of your journey and the landscape of your experience. Freed from the constraints of simple profits or traditional employment only, you can sow your seed towards pursuing your passions, exploring your interests, cultivating multiple streams of income, diversifying your financial portfolio, and enhancing your resilience in the face of economic uncertainty.

It is in your mindset you reject the notion of victimhood and embrace the limitless potential of human creativity and ingenuity. It is in your mindset that you unlock the boundless potential that lies dormant within, transcending limitations, and illuminating the path toward enterprise and fulfillment. It is in your mindset that you dream of and view your future venture through the lens of possibility, determination, and growth.

On this road, the effectual power of a changed mindset cannot be overemphasized. It shapes or reshapes many factors that drive you beyond the trickles of basic supply and propel you into the strata of multiplication and exponential dynamics right ahead.

So pay attention.

This road is littered with signs, divine hints, inspired nudges, and wisdom whispers. Do not speed past them. Let them tutor your thinking. Let them reroute your traffic from survival to dominion.

> **Road sign 1**: **Circumstances Don't Define You**. Along this route, it is not the circumstances you face that define you, but the mindset with which you interpret and face them. Rather than being bound by external circumstances or societal expectations, as is the norm on the path to poverty, you can chart your own course along the road to riches, guided by your deepest passions, values, and aspirations. No

matter what's happening around you, you still carry power within, power to shift how you see, power to change what you believe, power to act deliberately. You can magnetize opportunities. You can attract resources. You can call abundance by name. And yes, you can build a life of purpose and fulfillment, right where you are. A shaky mindset sees problems everywhere. A steady mindset sees challenges to overcome. But a strong mindset? It sees opportunities hidden in plain sight. With the right mindset, you can transform adversity into opportunity and pave the way for a future brimming with possibility and promise.

Road sign 2: **You're Powerful, Your Seed is Potent**. You have read that God gives us the power to get wealth. Yes, He does, and even much more. God gives you power to get wealth and then provides you with seed. He gave seed with force, seed with future, seed with heaven's algorithm for multiplication and exponential buried deep within it. But there is a mystery: He leaves you as the sole administrator of the given power, how it is harnessed, and how the forces within your seed are deployed towards creation, addition, and exchange of value. The poor pockets or diverts his power, consumes his seed with its in-built potential, and then starts seeking financial miracles elsewhere. On this road, you've got to channel your power properly and employ the forces of your seed correctly. If you don't, you head back to where consumption never ceases and yet never satisfies, to where appetite is endless, but fulfillment is extinct.

Road sign 3: **Nobody ever got rich by shouting "Hallelujah" or saying "Amen!":** No one ever prospered by echoing a thousand "Amen" while their hands remained idle and their fields untended. You won't either, no matter how loud yours sounds. You can cry in tongues, dance in fire, roll on the floor, but if you bring no value, you will harvest no increase. "Amen" without exchanging value is like waiting to harvest a field that you allowed to be overgrown with weeds. It is important to fine-tune your mindset to accept that genuine success comes from the value we bring to the table. A seed left unsown, though prayed over, will still rot. A field left untouched, though fasted for, will still grow weeds. God blesses the work of your hands, not just the vibrations of your voice. He breathes on what you build, offer, and exchange, not what you merely declare. So understand: Every time you create value, solve a problem, meet a need, birth a solution, you are echoing "Amen" in the spirit realm. You are saying, "Let it be so" to the gift God has placed inside you. Every act of value is a prophetic agreement with heaven. And when your value touches others, the harvest will find you.

Road sign 4: **Financial Miracle lives inside your Seed**. God keeps more financial miracles inside of your seed-power and your gift-power than you can ever find in lucky breaks, lotteries, found money, money doubling, or get-rich-quick schemes. It lives in your seed. It breathes in your gift. So, here on this road, it is an aberration to claim financial miracles when you have eaten your seed and neglected your gifting.

Your gift-power and seed-power combine efforts to help you create, add or multiply value and, subsequently, sustained wealth.

Road sign 5: **Money Follows Value without Discrimination**. People exchange money for value everywhere under the sun. Money has no favourite. It does not bow to titles, tongues, or tradition. It follows value, like a shadow to light. Wherever there is something meaningful, transformational, or desirable, money will move in its direction. The market does not ask about your tribe. It asks for your values. It does not check your denomination. It checks your delivery. Value is scalable. You can serve one value to many in one place. You can serve more value to more people in more places. But the equation never changes: more value equals more flow. When you multiply value, money has no choice but to follow.

Road sign 6: **Salary Only? Not Enough for Kingdom Riches**. No man enters kingdom wealth on salary alone. Wages were never designed to carry mantles. Fixed income cannot unlock generational transfer. Those who touch the dimension of kingdom riches do not depend on one stream. They understand that salary is Layer One, basic provision, not final destination. But wealth requires layered flow; from streams, channels, systems, and fields. If you're waiting for salary to make you rich, you're waiting for a bucket to flood a city. It won't. It can't. It never was meant to. You must build more. Trade more. Steward more. And stretch your hands wide enough to catch what heaven is releasing. Because kingdom riches are not accidental; they are administered.

Road sign 7: **Needed: Multiple Sources of Value Exchange.**
Some people call this Multiple Streams of Income, but I call it Multiple Sources of Value Exchanging. They are the same in the kingdom economy, because money bows to usefulness. Money follows the exchange of value in every nation on earth. The currency of heaven is value, and money is simply the earth's response to value exchanged. No one who truly has his hands on kingdom riches depends on only one source of income. You must position yourself at the intersection of creation, addition, and delivery of value. If you cannot yet build your own product, partner with one. If you cannot yet invent, innovate upon what already exists. And if you cannot yet create or add, then become a divine courier in the value chain. Deliver value from those who have it to those who need it. Whether it is many products in one place or one product in many places, or many versions of the same product in many places, as long as value moves, wealth flows. This is how you build streams, not through leakages. This is how you dig wells, not with wishes.

Road sign 8: **Making Money Differs from Managing or Multiplying Money**. Making money is dramatically different from managing money. Making money is also not the same as multiplying money. To truly have access to kingdom storehouses, voyagers must learn to make money, manage money, and multiply money. Many people live life hoping for some huge, miraculous money that will solve all their money problems. Too many are chasing new jobs, new salaries, or miracle cheques from the clouds, as if the next dollar is their deliverer. It is an illusion because it just doesn't happen like that. You've got to practice money management and multiplication principles with whatever you are earning if you must grow rich. Otherwise, you will repeat the same cycle in a new suit, on a different desk, and under a different title. You can make fast money by playing football or winning the lottery, for example–those are the kinds of miracle money many people are hoping for. So many ex-players who once played for big clubs and earned millions of dollars in the process have ended up in poverty because they made money but could not manage or multiply it. Many lottery winners have also been known to end up being poor a few years after winning jackpots, because money came, but mastery never did. You don't become rich by what you make. You become rich by what you multiply. Making money is important; it gives you a glimpse of what could be for you and your children. But managing and multiplying money are two protocols that establish you in kingdom riches. Without following these protocols, everyone who gets into money soon becomes "formerly rich." The good news is that you can start managing and multiplying money from wherever you are along the road to riches. Managing money begins with separating your seed, but doesn't end there; multiplying money begins with seizing opportunities to sow your separated seed in fertile soil. This is the intersection of the three unbreakable laws.

Road sign 9: **The Mind Sees Opportunities before the Eyes.**

Great opportunities are not first seen with the eyes, but with the mind. The boundless potential inherent in your seed is not observable with the lens, but with the mind. The greatest visionaries did not wait for evidence. They built with imagination and saw with the mind what the eyes could not yet verify. When you have 2 seeds and eat the 2 seeds, it is not only the two devoured seeds that are gone forever, but all possible future plantations and potential forests. In those seeds lived plantations. And in those plantations lived forests. And in those forests were streams of wealth unspeakable. But with a kingdom mind, you see differently. You see your 2 seeds multiplied by 9 (for example) becoming 18, or your 2 seeds raised to the power of 9 becoming 512, not by magic, but by sowing, watering, and trusting biblical principles to do what calculators cannot. The 2 seeds don't look like 18 or 512 unless you can envision them first, through the mind, and then sow them in a proven field to actualize what the mind has seen. And until your mind can see it, your hand won't plant it. And until your hand plants it, heaven won't multiply it. So train your mind to see beyond Layer One. For in the depths of your imagination lies the blueprint for your next elevation.

2nd **Interchange:**

Informational/Instructional Signs: Change Your Focus on Income Generation

Another key difference noticeable along the express lane to kingdom riches is that the wise voyager learns to shift from sweating for every coin to sowing for continuous flow. Voyagers set their focus on channels that multiply and compound their income regularly, sometimes with little or no personal sweat or physical presence. Instead of their sweat, their seeds do much of the work required to bring a regular income to them. At the beginning, yes, there may be byways that demand your hands, your time, and your sweat. You may work jobs that bring only dew, trickles, not torrents. But the seasoned voyager knows: this is not the destination. It's just a staircase. So they plant even while sweating. They serve even in hidden places. They learn while earning in drops. Whatever happens now, their bull's eye is set on the expressway that amplifies their effort and income down the road. They do not despise the dewdrops. They use it to water their foundation. They turn every droplet into discipline and every step into structure that builds more formidable brooks of value creation or addition. That's the covenant: your seed was pre-designed to sweat so you don't have to do so for so long. And when you deploy it with wisdom, you build not just income, but conduits of perpetual increase.

What do rich voyagers focus on?

There are three categories of channels that voyagers set their focus on as they travel along the road to riches:

Informational/Instructional Sign 1: Focus on Growth-Inducing Income Channels. Not every platform is for pampering. Some are for pruning. Some assignments are not meant to fill your pockets, but to forge your person. These are growth-inducing income channels, the humble beginnings of many kingdom voyagers. They may look like common jobs, small contracts, modest stipends, or internships with no applause, but they are divine scaffolds for greater things. They don't necessarily pay much, but they pay off. These channels help you learn, grow, and develop a network.

> **To Learn:** You come here not just to earn, but to learn. You come here to sit at the feet of process, to watch systems and control measures at work, to touch the inner mechanics of enterprise and excellence.
>
> **To Grow:** You come to grow your skills, your discipline, and your capacity on both the technical side and the business side of kingdom business.
>
> **To Develop:** You come to build networks, endurance, credibility, and future leverage.

Here, salaries are stepping stones, not destinations. Allowances are seeds, not crowns. Bonuses are dewdrops, not rain. And yes, the hours may be long, and the compensation low, but the reward, which is who you are becoming in the process, is far richer than the paycheck.

These channels don't look like much, but they birth men and women who can be trusted with more. These are the vessels that Heaven often uses to test your stewardship, stretch your vision, and train your hands for war in the economy of the Kingdom.

Common Features of Growth-Inducing Income Channels

　　i. They may mirror regular jobs, but it's the mindset that turns them into launchpads.
　　ii. The pay may be basic, and the bonuses scarce, but its purpose is to build, not pamper.
　　iii. Increments come not in streams but in trickles of addition, extras, and add-ons. However, they train the voyager to gather little by little.
　　iv. They provide avenues for voyagers to learn and develop valuable skill-sets quickly. They are bootcamps of wisdom, schools of value, and fast-tracks to skill.
　　i. And once you pass through these channels, you will stand, not as a beggar for opportunity, but as a builder of legacy.

So don't curse the small door. Walk through it with passion, because sometimes, the road to riches begins in rooms where nothing looks rich, except the future inside you.

Key examples:

i. Apprenticeships & Internships – not just learning, but laying foundations for dominion
ii. Small Businesses – planted with mustard seeds, destined to become trees
iii. Salaries + Shares – not just income, but ownership training wheels
iv. Hourly Wages – time converted into trust
v. Freelance Income – streams formed by skill
vi. Commissions – reward tied to your reach
vii. Tips & Gratuities – honor given in coins
viii. Bonuses & Overtime – due from diligence
ix. Pension or Retirement – past seeds still speaking

There is nothing wrong with starting small. But practically everything is wrong about staying small. The mindset of smallness builds tiny rooms and calls them destiny. It sees smallness, expects smallness, reaches for smallness, and always hits its target. But here on this road, you dare not shrink. You dare not stay small, because what lies within your current income, whether salary, tip, or trickle, is a seed packed with command and saturated with multiplication and exponential forces. You may hold a paycheck that feels like crumbs, but if you see through kingdom eyes, you'll recognize: this crumb contains a code for multiplication. Don't judge your seed by its size; judge it by its Source.

Informational/Instructional Sign 2: Focus on Capital Gains Income Channels: There is a kind of income that doesn't sweat daily; but it grows silently. It doesn't shout, but it compounds. It is the profit that rises not from motion, but from positioning: and it is called Capital Gains. It refers to the increase in value of an asset or investment with time. You don't sell immediately; you wait. You don't chase quick applause; you plant and hold. And when time matures what wisdom has chosen, you harvest the difference as gain. Focusing on capital gains is central to profiting from your assets and accumulating wealth with time.

There are two far-sighted lanes in this realm:

i. <u>Short-Term Capital Gains</u>: These are gains on the assets you hold for one year or less. They are typically taxed at the individual's ordinary income tax rate. They come quickly, get taxed heavily, and teach speed but not necessarily strategy.

ii. <u>Long-term Capital Gains</u>: These gains are realized from your assets held for more than a year and are normally taxed at a lower rate than ordinary income, which provides a significant tax advantage for voyagers. They are birthed through patience, taxed lightly, and backed by the wisdom of "he who endures shall be rewarded."

What types of assets generate capital gains and whisper wealth over time? Wise Voyagers often hold a diverse portfolio of assets that could generate capital gains, including:

- Stocks: Buying shares of companies that rise with the tide of progress.
- Real Estate: Purchasing properties that appreciate even while you sleep.
- Businesses: Investing in or owning private companies that grow cities.
- Collectibles and Art: Investing in rare items that speak value across generations, whose value can significantly appreciate in due course.
- Cryptocurrency: Buying digital assets, led by wisdom, and profiting from their volatile price increases.

Road Sign 3: Focus on Residual Income Channels: This is a type of income that does not beg for your daily sweat. It does not knock at your door each morning, asking for labour. It flows; even when you're resting. It gathers, even while you're worshiping. It is called residual income, and it is not just financial wisdom; it is a prophetic advantage. It is the kind of wealth that whispers:

"You once sowed. Now watch it grow."

It's the income that keeps speaking long after your mouth has closed, your yesterday's obedience still funding today's harvest. Wise voyagers on the road to kingdom riches don't ignore these streams. They position, prepare, and plant; then let time and structure carry the flow. Residual income isn't just smart. It is multiplication in motion.

Types of Residual Income:

1. Investment Income: When money breeds money

- ➢ Dividends from stocks: Where your ownership in enterprises becomes a monthly source of returns. These stocks provide regular dividend payments, which are portions of a company's earnings distributed to shareholders. In due course, these dividends can provide a significant source of residual income.
- ➢ Bonds and Interest: Where your capital becomes your servant, working in boardrooms you never enter. Public bonds, corporate bonds, and other fixed-income securities are popular among voyagers for their steady income streams.
- ➢ Mutual Funds and ETFs: Pools of potential, managed by wisdom, paying you back in portions for your patience. By investing in mutual funds and exchange-traded funds (ETFs), voyagers can receive distributions that can serve as residual income.
- ➢ Etc.

2. Real Estate Income: Let the land work

- ➢ Rental Properties: Bricks and mortar become streams and manna, as tenants unknowingly fund your journey. Smart voyagers often hire property managers to handle day-to-day operations, making the income truly passive.

- Real Estate Investment Trusts (REITs): This is real estate, without the burden. It's a seat at the property table without lifting a brick. They allow investors to buy shares in a portfolio of real estate assets. REITs typically pay out most of their income as dividends, providing a regular income stream without the need to manage properties directly.
- Etc.

3. Intellectual Property: Legacy that pays in echoes

- Royalties from Books, Music, and Patents: Every note composed, every book penned, every invention birthed, still pays down the pike. Authors, musicians, and inventors earn royalties from their creative works and inventions.
- Franchising: Franchisees pay ongoing royalties to the franchisor based on a percentage of sales, helping voyagers to earn residual income by franchising their businesses. Your business becomes a blueprint; others follow, and you still receive the blessing.
- Etc.

4. Business Income

- Silent Partnerships and Equity Stakes: Voyagers invest in businesses as silent partners or take equity stakes without being involved in daily operations. You fund the vision; they run the race, and the profits still find you.

- Online Businesses: E-commerce stores, digital products, and membership sites can generate residual income. Systems that don't sleep, products that keep giving, while you raise families and steward nations. Click by click, download by download, abundance flows in silence.
- Etc

Residual income is not just a smart option. It is kingdom wisdom for dominion. It's how the diligent rest, how the wise multiply. So, build your streams. Dig your wells. And let your yesterday keep paying your tomorrow. Because in the Kingdom, it's not just about what you earn… It's about what keeps earning when you no longer can.

3rd Interchange:

Warning Signs: Delayed Gratification Is Never Outdated

In a world addicted to now, in an age of immediate pleasures, cravings are crowned kings and patience is mocked as weakness. And the concept of waiting for rewards has almost become archaic. Fast food, instant streaming, and same-day delivery have cultivated an expectation of immediate results. However, in building lasting wealth on this road, delayed gratification is not just a quaint notion from a bygone era; it is a fundamental principle for financial success. It is deeply carved into the architecture of the kingdom's wealth.

Delayed gratification refers to the ability to resist the temptation of an immediate reward in preference for a later, often greater, reward. Delayed gratification is not about self-deprivation; it is about making choices today that could lead you to greater rewards tomorrow. The road to riches is long, but with patience and discipline, it is a journey well worth taking.

These days, we scroll, we click, we consume, faster than we discern. But here on this road, the wise don't eat every fruit in season. They save seed. They endure hunger now so they can host a harvest later. They master the art of restraint, because they understand this one unshakable truth: You must not feast today on what's meant to fund your future.

Delayed gratification will help you:

- **Warning Sign 1–Improve Financial Discipline**: Every "no" to a passing pleasure is a "yes" to generational provision. Developing the habit builds financial discipline and makes it easier to stick to budgets and financial plans.
- **Warning Sign 2–** Starve the impulse, feed the future. Shun unnecessary spending to prioritize savings and investment.
- **Warning Sign 3–Kill The Debt Beast Before It Kills Your Destiny**. Debt is a master that makes slaves of kings. Pay off debts faster and avoid high-interest costs. It teaches you to wait for what you own instead of borrowing what will own you.

> **Warning Sign 4**-**Simple Interest is an Enemy of Compounding**: Every dollar sown and left to grow is a sermon in compound interest. The voyager who resists consumption today will receive a crown of compounded reward tomorrow.

> **Warning Sign 5**- **Castles Are Not Built Overnight**: You cannot save for a house, a legacy, a life that matters, if your wallet bleeds at every checkout counter. Delayed gratification makes dreams affordable and divine promises reachable.

So, hold your hunger. Train your taste. Silence the craving that wants it all now. Because, on this road, what you delay today could become what delivers you tomorrow. The foolish demand fire without gathering wood, but the wise stack logs in patience. And when their season comes, they burn brighter than anyone ever imagined.

Build Your Field First–Then Your House

Almost everywhere you turn today, appearance screams louder than substance. Many chase symbols of success–cars, homes, luxury–before laying a solid foundation. But Biblical wisdom whispers differently. Proverbs 24:27 counsels:

> "Prepare your work outside; get everything ready for yourself in the field, and after that build your house." (ESV) Look at that verse in simpler versions:

"First get your fields ready, next plant your crops, and then build your house." (ERV)

"Develop your business first before building your house." (TLB)

In other words:

> Gather the oil before you light the lamp.
> Build the well before you draw the water.
> Grow the roots before you chase the fruit.
> Anchor the vision before you sail the vessel.
> Secure the flow before you build the fountain.
> Train your hands before you wield the crown.
> Fund the future before you furnish the present.
> Lay the foundation before you paint the dream.

There are men in this kingdom, strategic, patient, princely in thought, who delay the keys to dream homes not because they are broke, but because they are builders first. They know the divine order: assets before aesthetics, substance before scenery, the field before the facade.

This is not about rejecting comfort. It's about refusing to be trapped by it. They could fund the house, furnish the rooms, and install the marble... But they chose, instead, to sow into streams that will water generations. They understand that you don't harvest from a kitchen, you harvest from a field, unless the kitchen is your field. And if the field is ignored while the house is worshipped, the rains will stop showing up.

Too many today live in palaces that pay them nothing. They are house-rich, but future-poor. They put granite counters above scalable ventures, living in a dream house they can't sustain. They're chest of vanity, but crucify cash-flow. They sleep on Egyptian cotton while their future bleeds at the altar of premature comfort.

The lesson is simple:

Don't build your house with your sweat. Build the field that will build your house. Let your field work for you before your house defines you. Delay the showroom to fund the workshop. Delay the decor to fund the dominion. Postpone the parade until the pillars are proven.

Because when your field flows, your house will flourish. And when your foundation is strong, no storm can crack your peace. This is wisdom. This is how kings build.

4th Interchange:

Regulatory (Mandatory) Signs: Separate and Sow Your Seed

Check out the following verses of the Bible

> Then Isaac sowed in that land, and reaped in the same year a hundredfold; and the Lord blessed him.

> The man began to prosper, and continued prospering until he became very prosperous; Genesis 26:12-13 NKJV.

This is not poetic repetition; this is divine progression. This is the protocol of increase unveiled in holy sequence.

Kindly read those lines again. Observe that the verses flawlessly align with layers 1, 2, and 3 of the principles of God's provision?

- The man, Isaac, sowed
- Then he **began** to prosper
- And **continued** to prosper
- Until he **became** very prosperous

This is no accident. This is God's threefold economy on full display:

- Layer 1: Initiation.
- Layer 2: Continuity.
- Layer 3: Overflow.

Notice: Isaac's prosperity didn't fall from the sky. It grew from a seed. It wasn't overnight. It was over layers. From the soil of obedience, the cycle of wealth began. From one act of sowing, a rhythm of increase was born.

This is not just an isolated testimony. It's a template.

Now, where do you think Isaac got the seed he sowed before he **began to prosper?**

Let's take the liberty of assuming likely scenarios, using contemporary possibilities:

- He could have sown the seed he kept from the previous harvest, or
- He could have purchased seed with the money he saved from previous sales, or
- He could have borrowed seed from people who lent to him at some interest.

No man can reach "very prosperous" on salary alone. You must partner with the process, walk the layers, and honor the rhythm.

Sowing time and harvest are ageless principles that no alternative can overrule, irrespective of location and time. In the same way, growing riches also abide by biblical principles:

- <u>**Regulatory Sign 1**</u>: **Mobilize your seed**–separated from previous harvest, purchased from previous sale, or borrowed from your network
- <u>**Regulatory Sign 2**</u>: **Prepare your field**–venture or investment
- <u>**Regulatory Sign 3**</u>: **Sow your seed**–and till your ground
- <u>**Regulatory Sign 4**</u>: **Wait patiently** afterward
- <u>**Regulatory Sign 5**</u>: **Harvest your field**

- **Regulatory Sign 6: Separate your seed** from your bread
- **Regulatory Sign 7: Repeat** the process

I have seen it too many times. Men and women claim Isaac's harvest, yet eat what Isaac would have sown. I have seen many people fruitlessly wait to receive multiple-fold blessings simply because they donated to their pastors, with no sown field! They lift their hands to claim a hundredfold return, but swallow their seeds on the altar of self-indulgence. They expect divine multiplication from empty fields. They expect kingdom economics to respond to emotion, not obedience.

Let it be shouted from the watchtowers: God is not a magician. He is a God of principle, a God of patterns, a God of protocols. The principles of His provision are both unbendable and inviolable along this voyage. Multiplication is not a mystery; it is a law. Multiplication and exponential increase only trail a separated seed that is sown on fertile ground. And they bend to no one.

Donation is not sowing. Tipping a pastor is not a substitute for planting in fertile ground. Your applause in church, your "Amen!" at conferences, your generous gifts to men of God, they fertilize the soil, yes. They water the field, yes. But they cannot substitute the seed itself.

On this road, there are no shortcuts. Every voyager must reckon with the inviolable order of provision: Today's separated seed is the womb of tomorrow's abundance. Eat the seed, and you abort the future. Swallow it in the name of survival, and you'll find yourself soliciting in the season of surplus.

No matter how loud your declaration, no matter how sincere your worship, there is no harvest without a seed. And there is no lasting wealth for those who consume what was meant to be planted. Let the voyagers beware: harvest only follows hands that sow, and the riches of tomorrow only bloom from what you're willing to bury today.

5th Interchange:

Landmark Signs: Lookout for opportunities

Look out! Opportunities don't always knock. Sometimes, you've got to track them down. You want to grow your income? Then stop waiting for "luck" and start looking for landmarks. The journey to riches is marked by signs, not just street signs, but knowledge signs, discipline signs, and action signs. Here are 10 such signs pointing you toward investment opportunities that match your goals and risk appetite.

i. **<u>Landmark Sign 1</u>– Self-Education Is Non-Negotiable**: Money doesn't stay long with the ignorant. If you don't know how wealth works, it won't work for you. Read books. Take courses. Listen to financial podcasts. Follow people who are doing what you hope to do. Learn the language of money.

ii. **Landmark Sign 2–Set Clear Financial Goals**: Set your financial GPS. Are you aiming for early retirement? Passive income? Wealth for your children? Without clear goals, your investments lack focus, and scattered focus doesn't grow sturdy trees.

iii. **Landmark Sign 3–Tap into Online Investment Platforms**: Technology has democratized access to investment opportunities. Use it. Convenience is not the enemy, ignorance is. Explore platforms like:

- Stock Trading: E*TRADE, Robinhood, TD Ameritrade
- Robo-Advisors: Betterment, Wealthfront
- Real Estate Crowdfunding: Fundrise, RealtyMogul

iv. **Landmark Sign 4–Real Estate Still Reigns**: From REITs to rentals to fractional ownership, real estate remains a time-tested wealth generator. You don't need to own the entire building, just start with a brick.

v. **Landmark Sign 5–Invest in People Who Invest**: Join investment groups. Attend local or virtual meetups. Connect with those who have done what you want to do. Some of the best investment tips come wrapped in conversations, not just data.

vi. **Landmark Sign 6–Get in the Room**: Workshops, bootcamps, masterclasses, they're not just for learning. They're for access. Often, the real ROI isn't the slides, it's who you shake hands with.

vii. **Landmark Sign 7– Spread Your Net, Not Your Neck**: Mitigate risk by spreading investments across asset classes. Diversify. Don't put all your eggs, or ego, in one basket. Balance growth and income. Learn about alternative investments. Look into investments outside traditional stocks and bonds, such as

- Cryptocurrencies (e.g., Bitcoin, Ethereum etc)
- Commodities (e.g., gold, silver, oil)
- Collectibles (e.g., art, rare coins, vintage assets)

The more seasoned you are in alternative investments, the wider your opportunity lens becomes.

viii. **Landmark Sign 8–<u>Ride the Waves, Don't Be Drowned by Them</u>**: Stay informed about market trends. Stay ahead of trends. Track market movements. Know what the economy is whispering, and sometimes screaming, to identify potential investment opportunities. Tools like MarketWatch, Bloomberg, and Yahoo Finance should be part of your daily diet..

ix. **<u>Landmark Sign 9–Don't Just Guess. Get Guidance</u>**: A seasoned financial advisor won't just crunch numbers; they'll calibrate your risk, challenge your assumptions, and help you see around corners.

x. **<u>Landmark Sign 10– Your Network Is a Treasure Map:</u>** Leverage your existing network: Tell people you're ready to invest. Let your circle know you're not just saving, but scaling. Opportunity often wears the face of someone you already know.

Wealth rewards the watchful. Opportunities don't sparkle on the surface. You uncover them when you become the kind of person who attracts them. So, don't just look around, look within, look ahead, and look again.

6th Interchange:

Traffic/Lane Management Signs: Do Your Homework.

Smart voyagers don't gamble with their seed. They don't chase rumours, whispers, or barbershop forecasts when deciding where to invest. Instead, they break up their fallow ground, they dig deep, learn, question, and discern before they ever release a single coin.

Research every investment opportunity before investing. If you don't understand where your money is going, what drives the returns, what risks are hiding, how the charges work, or what the endgame looks like, you're not investing, you're just donating your destiny to chance. The scripture is very clear about this, admonishing those who choose to travel this road, that:

> Break up your fallow ground, **and do not sow among thorns.** Jer. 4:3b (KJV)

This is not just spiritual advice. It's financial wisdom. Don't let a friend, a flashy testimonial, or a persuasive uncle lead you blindly into a pit dressed like a promise. Even when others claim to "know the ropes," their knowledge cannot substitute for your understanding. You cannot bank on their knowledge alone to make investment decisions. Word-of-mouth should prompt research, not reckless action.

Why Research? Because your seed is sacred. It deserves to be placed with precision.

Deep research uncovers:

- How the investment works – the blueprint, the mechanics, the return cycle.
- What risks lie beneath – economic shifts, industry regulations, hidden fees.
- What the real upside looks like – not hype, but hard facts.
- Whether it aligns with your long-term purpose – not every opportunity is your opportunity.

If you don't want to throw your seed away, if you don't want to squander your investment, you need to have a good understanding of the specifics of any venture before investing. Understand the company. Investigate the sector. Learn the terrain. Ask hard questions. If it sounds too good, dig deeper. If it looks too smooth, scratch the surface.

In the world of investing, ignorance is expensive, and wisdom is wealth. To make better judgments, you must be able to identify potential risks and pitfalls associated with your investment. Knowing the downsides helps you develop strategies to mitigate risks and protect your capital.

Knowing the long-term prospects of a business, its ability to innovate and adapt to market-changes, ensures that you invest in companies that are likely to grow and succeed rather than in hype-driven bubbles. This discipline will protect your seed from being scattered on thorns and ensure it lands on good soil, soil that multiplies, not misleads.

7th Interchange:

Incident/Work Zone Signs: Don't Just Store the Seed: Sow It

You've done your due diligence. You've separated your seed. You've broken up your fallow ground. But here's the truth: no matter how carefully you guard a seed, it won't multiply until it's planted. Wisdom without action is potential without purpose.

Your seed was never meant to sit in a safe. It was designed to enter the soil, disappear for a season, and rise again, transformed. The act of sowing is what activates the promise of the seed. Without it, all your preparation becomes procrastination dressed as prudence.

> Sow your seed in the morning and do not be idle with your hands in the evening, for you do not know whether morning or evening planting will succeed, whether this or that, or whether both alike will be good. Ecclesiastes 11:6 AMP.

So don't stall.

Sow in the morning, when clarity is fresh, and faith is sharp. Sow in the evening, when fatigue tempts you to fold your hands and wait for certainty. Because in this kingdom economy, you don't need perfect timing to see fruitful returns; you need obedience and consistency.

Whether in business, investment, generosity, or innovation, the seed you refuse to sow is the harvest you'll never see.

So go ahead. Sow it.

Risk the death of the seed, and trust in the resurrection of reward.

Areas to invest in

Incident/Work Zone Sign 1–Invest in Yourself: The first and most powerful place to invest is not the stock market. Not real estate. Not even a business. It is your mind. This is key because every tent, every future income stream, business, brand, or building, starts as an invisible structure within.

The Bible says:

> Enlarge the place of thy tent, and let them stretch out the curtains of thine dwelling: Do not spare, Lengthen thy cords, And strengthen thy stakes. Isaiah 54:2 (NKJV).

Did you notice that there are four areas that need to be enlarged, strengthened, or made bigger? It doesn't begin with structures, materials, or plots of land. It began with the place of your tent.

Let's break it down:

- The place of your tent – Your mind, your internal world, your thinking patterns.
- The curtains – Your outward expressions: habits, routines, discipline.
- The cords – Your connections, relationships, collaborations.
- The stakes – Your convictions, character, and the non-negotiables that anchor your life.

Let me talk about **"the place of your tent"** in this section. The first and primary "place of your tent", which needs to be enlarged, is not on the plot of land where your tent (or investment) is sited or expected to be sited, but in your mind. The primary place is in your mind, while the secondary place is on the plot of land itself. Before a skyscraper ever kissed the skyline, it lived first in the mind. And before that thought ever becomes visible, it materialized in the mind of a designer. It was sketched out on paper drawing. It was turned into a blueprint, 3D schema, for others to interpret, understand, and build. The designer conceived a multi-story building and later transferred the 'tower' in his mind from the mental to the physical realm. Likewise, your mind is the construction site for your destiny. If all you can imagine is a bungalow, don't expect a tower to rise on your behalf.

You must also start developing your mind (the primary place for your life's superstructure) to conceive, design, or transform your own value creation production lines or value addition ventures, even if you are still a salary earner. After the mental tower comes its physical construct.

It is breath-taking to know that anyone can grow! You must invest in yourself, because capacity comes before capital. It will grow your capability to earn more money, manage money, manage people, manage projects, manage other resources, and steward time and relationships. No one was born with mastery over these. But everyone can develop them

If entrepreneurship currently intimidates you, that's proof your mind needs enlarging. Otherwise, it will terrify you in real life. If business ownership terrorizes your brainpower, if long-term investment frightens your mentality, that's a signal, not of failure, but of the next level of investment required: in YOU. If not, they will bully you in the physical. Entrepreneurship skills can be learned. Competency in business management can be grown. If you don't stretch internally, you'll remain limited externally.

Major Stopover Sign: After miles and miles of endless road stretching before you, personal development should always be taken as a stop sign. At some points on this long, unrelenting highway—after the deadlines, the detours, and the dizzying speed of survival— there comes a timely sign:

STOP. This brief, commanded rest becomes an unexpected gift before you press on. It's not delay. It's divine instruction. A moment where the engine of ambition goes quiet and breath returns like a long-lost friend. This pause isn't punishment; it's preparation. It's a reminder that any destination matters less than the ability to truly arrive. Growth doesn't happen at 120 km/h. It happens in stillness: in that holy hush where you realign, refocus, and refuel.

There are time-tested ways to grow. There are simple, solid strategies that stretch you personally and professionally. And when you practise them consistently, they change everything.

- Sharpen your tools – Develop skills that speak to where you're going, not just where you've been.
- Feed Your Mind – Read deeply. Listen wisely. Let fresh insight interrupt your assumptions.
- Learn On Purpose – Courses, coaching, curiosity, make learning a lifestyle, not a chore.
- Strengthen Your Circle – Surround yourself with voices that see your future and speak to your becoming.
- Submit to Mentorship – Let those who've walked ahead hand you a lantern for your path.
- Master Your Money – Learn to steward resources with wisdom so that lack never hijacks your calling.

Don't miss your stop. You're not just traveling, you're transforming. And every true transformation demands a pause.

Incident/Work Zone Sign 2–**Invest in Business Income**: The second area to invest is in business income. You weren't wired just to collect paychecks, you were born to create value and multiply it. One of the wisest places to plant your seed is in a business income stream. Why? Because business gives you the power to serve many while securing your freedom.

1. **Start Something Online:** The internet has levelled the field. Anyone with values can build a venture. Here are a few seeds you can plant:
    - E-commerce stores – Sell physical or digital goods.
    - Online courses & coaching – Teach what you know.
    - Freelancing & consulting – Get paid for your expertise.
    - Content creation – Build a platform and monetize your voice.
    - SaaS (Software as a Service) – Create apps that solve problems.
    - Print on Demand, Dropshipping – Sell without inventory.
    - Subscription/membership sites – Build a loyal community.
    - E-books & publishing – Package your knowledge.
    - Domain flipping – Buy low, sell high in the digital real estate world.

2. **Start a Traditional Business:** If you love brick-and-mortar or physical operations, there's room for you too:
    a. Sole Proprietorship – You run the show solo.
    b. Partnerships – Team up to share risk and reward.
        i. General, Limited, or Silent, you choose the dynamic.
        ii. LLC (Limited Liability Company) – You get flexibility and protection.
        iii. Silent Partnerships
    c. Corporation – Go bigger; attract investors, and separate personal from business finances.

3. **Buy an Existing Business**:–Skip the painful startup phase. Buy what's already working. But don't rush, do your homework. Study their books, brand, and customer trust before signing anything.

4. **Franchise a Brand**: – Want the freedom of business but with training wheels? A franchise gives you a proven system, support, and brand recognition, so you're building, but not from scratch.

5. **Form a Joint Venture**:–This is business teamwork, temporary or long-term. You combine forces, share the risk, and multiply impact. Think collaboration, not competition.

6. **Build or Join a Family Business**: – Family businesses aren't just about legacy; they're about shared purpose and generational wealth. Handle it with wisdom, structure, and clear roles.

7. **Grow Equity Where You Work (Employee Ownership)**:– Employees have significant ownership stakes in some businesses where employees acquire shares in due course, often as part of their compensation. It's called Employee Stock Ownership Plan (ESOP). Don't just clock in. Grow in. Some companies let you own a stake, you invest your years; they reward you with equity.

8. **Join or Start a Cooperative (Co-ops)**:– Want shared ownership, democratic decisions, and mutual benefit? Co-ops are common in agriculture, retail, and utilities, owned and operated by a group of individuals for their mutual benefit. Everyone wins, not just those at the top. Members share in profits and have a say in the decision-making process.

Business is more than hustle, it's your altar of impact. Choose the path that fits your calling, and build not just for income, but for influence, legacy, and kingdom expression.

Incident/Work Zone Sign 3–Invest in Capital Gain Channels: If you're serious about multiplying your money, not just adding to it but seeing it bloom in surprising folds, then you must learn to invest in a diverse portfolio of assets that can generate capital gains. Think of capital gains like planting trees instead of vegetables. Vegetables feed you now. Trees change the landscape and feed generations.

Here's the principle: you buy something of value, hold it wisely, and let time do the heavy lifting. Then one day, the market shifts, and what you bought for little becomes worth much more.

You can aim for:

- Short-Term Capital Gains: quick flips; you hold the asset for less than a year.
- Long-term Capital Gains: wealth with patience; held for over a year.

Some examples of assets generating capital gains include:

- Stocks – Owning small pieces of growing companies.
- Real Estate – Buying property and watching it appreciate with time.
- Businesses – Starting or investing in a venture that increases in value
- Collectibles and Art – Rare items that appreciate as they become harder to find.
- Cryptocurrency – Digital assets that rise and fall with bold waves.
- Forex Copy Trading or AI Trading Bots – Letting smarter systems or expert strategies trade on your behalf.

Capital gains don't shout loud like a salary; they whisper in due time. But if you listen and position well, they'll speak volumes in the future.

Major Stopover Sign: Proven Strategies for Maximizing Capital Gains

Capital gains are not just about buying low and selling high. They're about thinking long, positioning smart, and partnering wisely with time, insight, and strategy. If you're going to walk this road, here are proven strategies for harvesting more than you planted:

i. Embrace the Long Game: Patience isn't passive; it's power in disguise. Hold your investments long enough for them to mature and multiply. Long-term holds often enjoy friendlier tax rates, too.

ii. Diversify Like a Voyager: Don't put all your capital eggs in one basket, or even in one ship. Spread your investments across various asset classes and sectors. If some ships sink, one strong vessel can carry your entire fleet to shore.

iii. Partner with wisdom: Whether it's a seasoned advisor or a data-savvy portfolio manager, let informed minds help you steward your capital. Good counsel in investment is like wind to your sails; it multiplies your movement with less effort.

iv. Optimize for the Tax Man: Be smart with how and where you invest. Use tax-sheltered accounts. Harvest losses to offset gains.

Place your highest-growth assets where taxes take the smallest bite. Don't just make money; keep more of what you make.

v. Leverage, but Don't Gamble: Borrowing to invest can amplify your gains, if used with discipline and discernment. But never borrow to impress or indulge. Use leverage like a skilled archer uses tension: carefully, with precision, and only for the right target.

vi. Look beyond the Public Markets: Private equity and venture capital are where bold dreams become billion-dollar realities. Invest in startups or private firms that are solving real life problems. If they win, you win big. Sometimes the quietest seeds grow the loudest forests.

Capital gains are not luck. They are the rewards of strategy, foresight, and faithful waiting. Sow in wisdom. Hold with patience. Harvest in abundance.

Major Stopover Sign: Realizing and Reinvesting Capital Gains

Gaining wealth is only the beginning. What you do after you gain it determines if your harvest was a onetime miracle or the start of a multiplying cycle. Once your capital gains come in, don't just spend them. Replant. Redirect. Reinvest. That's how wealth flows instead of drying up.

Here's how to keep your gains working:

   a. Purchase More Assets: Buy more fruit-bearing trees, stocks, real estate, or anything else that appreciates in value. Don't just cash out, scale up. The best time to sow again is right after a harvest.
   b. Fund New Dreams: Let your gains become seed capital for new ventures. Invest in startups or launch businesses that solve real problems. This way, your gain becomes someone else's breakthrough, and possibly your next windfall.
   c. Give with Strategy: Philanthropy isn't just generosity, it's strategic stewardship. Create foundations, sponsor causes, or fund impact initiatives. Besides potential tax advantages, this helps your wealth echo into legacies.

Capital gains aren't the end of the story. They're the beginning of a new one, if you choose to reinvest with vision.

Incident/Work Zone Signs 4–Invest in Residual Income Channels: Residual income is money earned repeatedly from a single effort or investment. It's income that keeps flowing, even while you sleep. If you want to escape the trap of living paycheck to paycheck, this is where to look. Below are proven avenues for building residual income that can secure your financial future.

Examples of residual income to invest in

1. **Investment-Based Residual Income:** These are income streams that arise from putting your money to work through financial instruments. Here are some types:
    i. Interest Income: Earned from fixed-income instruments like savings accounts, bonds, and certificates of deposit (CDs).
    ii. Dividends: Payments received as a shareholder of stocks, mutual funds, or ETFs, directly tied to company profits.
    iii. Capital Gains: Profit made from selling assets like stocks, bonds, or real estate for more than their purchase price.
    iv. Rental Income: Steady earnings from leasing properties, equipment, vessels, or even industrial machinery.
    v. Annuities: A retirement-focused investment that provides consistent payouts with time.
    vi. Business or Private Equity Income: Earnings from partial ownership in a company; either passively as a silent partner or actively through venture capital.
    vii. Peer-to-Peer Lending:. Interest income from lending funds to others through online lending platforms.
    viii. Mutual Funds and ETFs: Portfolio-based returns from diversified holdings managed by financial institutions.

ix. Hedge Fund Profits: Advanced returns from professionally managed funds investing in multiple asset classes using strategic models.

x. Cryptocurrency Staking: Earn rewards by staking your digital coins to help validate transactions on blockchain networks..

2. Real Estate Income: Contrary to popular belief on the pathway to poverty, real estate isn't reserved for the wealthy. Thinking you must have millions to get started is one of poverty's loudest lies. There are many entry points, some requiring little more than wisdom and discipline:

i. Rental Properties: Residential or commercial properties leased for monthly income.

ii. Real Estate Investment Trust (REIT) Dividends: Returns from investing in REIT, which pool funds to invest in income-generating real estate.

iii. Capital Gains: Profits from selling real estate at a higher price than it was bought.

iv. Property Flipping: Buy, renovate, and resell homes for a quick turnaround profit.

v. Short-Term Rentals: Income from platforms like Airbnb or Vrbo for vacation or daily rentals.

vi. Lease Payments: Income from leasing land, offices, or industrial spaces.

vii. Real Estate Crowdfunding: Invest in real estate projects collectively through platforms, even with a small amount of capital.

viii. Real Estate Development: Profits from developing raw land or properties and selling them post-construction.

ix. Consulting and Management Fees: Earnings from offering property management or advisory services.

x. Raw Land Leasing: Lease bare land for farming, resource extraction, or commercial development.

3. **Intellectual Property & Royalty Income:** If you create or own valuable intellectual assets, you can earn income repeatedly from their use. Here's how creators, inventors, and entrepreneurs tap into this:

   i. Music Royalties: Paid to artists, songwriters, or producers when their songs are streamed, performed, or used commercially.

   ii. Book Royalties: Ongoing payments to authors from book sales or adaptation rights (films, audio, etc.).

   iii. Patent Royalties: Earnings from licensing patented technologies, inventions, or processes.

   iv. Trademark Royalties: Payments received for allowing companies to use a brand name, logo, or tagline.

   v. Franchise Royalties: Ongoing fees paid by franchisees to franchisors to use a business model and brand.

- vi. Oil, Gas, and Mineral Royalties: Income from allowing companies to extract natural resources from your land.
- vii. Film and Television Royalties: Residuals paid to actors, writers, or producers when shows or films are aired, streamed, or sold.
- viii. Software Licensing Royalties: Income from permitting individuals or businesses to use, install, or resell software.
- ix. Art & Photography Royalties: Earned from licensing your visuals for commercial or creative use, ads, books, products, etc.
- x. Copyright Royalties: Income from the use of copyrighted material, such as digital content, educational materials, or research papers.

Lay By Sign: Building Residual Income–Steps by Step

1. Educate Yourself First: Start by learning what residual income is. It is money that keeps coming in even after the work is done. Voyagers who grow wealth often study topics like money, property, and business to learn how to make this kind of income.

2. Set Clear Goals: Know what you want to achieve with your money. Having a clear goal will help you make the right choices and stay focused.

3. Start Small: Begin by investing in one or two residual income streams. You can buy stocks that pay you regularly, buy a small house to rent out,

or make digital products like eBooks or online courses. Starting small helps you learn and make better choices as you grow.

4. Grow Over Time: As initial investments generate income, use the money you make to build even more streams of income. Slowly expand into other areas to spread your risk and increase your chances of success.

5. Monitor and Improve: Keep an eye on your income sources. Make changes if something isn't working well or if your goals change. This will help keep your plan on track.

Major Stop Over Sign: Proven Strategies to Maximize Residual Income

1. Diversification: Spread It Out: Don't put all your eggs in one basket. Use different asset classes and income streams to earn money, like stocks, real estate, or online businesses. This helps you stay safe if one area doesn't do well.

2. Leveraging Technology: Let tech make things easier. For example, you can use apps to manage rental properties or websites to sell your digital products. Automation saves time and reduces stress.

3. Professional Management: Hire Experts: Sometimes it helps to get professionals like financial advisors, property managers or business consultants. They can help you grow your income and avoid costly mistakes.

4. Reinvestment Your Income: Take the money you earn and use it to make more. For example, if you earn dividends from stocks, use that money to buy more stocks. Or if you earn rent, save up to buy another property.

5. Be Smart about Taxes: Use legal ways to reduce how much tax you pay. This might include special savings accounts, using tax write-offs, or employing trusts and other vehicles to reduce tax liabilities on their income.

Chapter 14

Incremental Power of Sown Seed

Take the Plunge!

Once you have all the basics, take a step. Your seed should not stay in custody forever! You're never going to have all things in a perfect state before starting, anyway. Start with your first investment. Do business registrations. If you are starting up a business, prayerfully set a start date, tell those who should know about the date, and set the ball rolling. Print the handbills if necessary and send the invites. Where applicable and if it is required, start on a part-time basis while you are still in your paid employment.

What are you doing? You are casting your seed. Build the website. Buy the equipment. Get your garage ready. Rent the office space if needed. Buy and install the furniture and fittings. Advertise vacant positions. Collate applicants and set a date for their first interview. Conduct the interviews, agree terms and conditions, and set a resumption date. If you don't start, you're never going to take significant steps.

Take the plunge! The next quarter won't be perfect; neither will the next year, or the next 20 years!

It always seems somewhat difficult to cast your first seed from your comfort zone. You are not sure if you will be successful. Sometimes, it feels like you should fine tune your plan again, so you delay your seed and postpone the decision to take the required plunge. You keep postponing your resignation date over and over. You first add three months, then another three months. Before you know it, another year has passed.

What is my advice to you? Cast that seed! Otherwise, it remains a solitary grain in your custody! That investment opportunity may not be available much longer. That idea may stay in your head and die in your head. That plan may remain a business plan in your custody for yet another one or more years! Once your seeds and the soil are ready, you are going to have to get down in the dirt.

It is risky to cast your seed. But people are casting theirs anyway! Let me assure you that thousands of ventures were launched across the world yesterday. Some other thousands will be launched today, with yet some others hitting the launch pad tomorrow! Your seed will never grow if you keep it in custody! If you postpone till next week, some tens of thousands of ventures would have been birthed between now and then. While many of them will fail for various reasons, yours doesn't have to. That is one reason I took some time to discuss essential considerations for venture success.

Get in the dirt! Get in the dirt and stay in the dirt. Dirty jobs are dirty, but the money you earn from there is clean, and neat! Some people want to stay in white-collar jobs. They seem to like the 'dignity' of wearing suits and ties. Let me tell you, my dear voyager: there is nothing dignifying in corporate suits and ties while you are neck-deep in debt. The only thing that's dignifying is the impact you make, with or without a suit and tie.

You look tiny but have titanic potential. Your potential is enormous. Even you are incapable of telling the real extent of what your potential can become. But then, all your potential for impact remains dormant until your seed is cast in order to activate those inner fortes. You can start and grow ventures that impact families, communities, nations, and even the world; but not on your comfortable couch.

There are many people who attended training in order to kick-start an investment, an impactful venture, but who never implemented what they learnt. You can't imagine the number of people who write their resignation letters once, twice, or even three times in order to quit some engagements and start their businesses. But so many keep the letters in their drawers and bags for weeks and months. There are some who actually submitted their resignation letters but quickly withdrew them because of the fear of the unknown. That is why some make impact happen, some watch impact happen, and some whine as impact happens. The makers of impact are those who cast their seeds.

Let them go! It is in casting those seeds that you can see new life spring forth to shape lives, reshape our world, and sway real legacy.

How God blesses the seed that is sown

Take an unhurried look at our opening scripture again:

> **Now he that ministereth seed to the sower both minister bread for your food, and multiply your seed sown, and increase the fruits of your righteousness.** 2 Cor 9:10 (KJV)

Here, again, we see the different incremental factors that God applies to your sown seeds, if they are viable and the condition is right. It is the prerogative of The Lord of the harvest to determine the factor and extent of the harvest.

The Power of Addition

At the outset of any business or investment, the rewards are often linear. This is the time you start with small, consistent steps. This is the steady accumulation of knowledge, skills, and capital. It is the daily grind, the early mornings, and the late nights. Profits trickle in like droplets of rain, accumulating steadily but not dramatically. This is the power of addition; where each effort brings a measurable, incremental return.

- You make the first sale, the first investment.
- Your startup acquires customers one by one
- As a new investor, you add small amounts of capital periodically.
- As an entrepreneur, you streamline a process, mastering a new skill through experience, each lesson adding to your toolkit.

Each minor victory adds to the momentum, building a foundation of confidence and experience. Every addition lays the bricks of your enterprise, one by one. Focus on the present, celebrate these minor triumphs, and watch them coalesce into something substantial.

It is here that many give up, discouraged by the slow march of progress. But those who persist, those who endure, those who understand that small, steady steps pave a voyager's road to greatness, these are the ones who move forward to witness the next level of growth.

The Magic of Multiplication

The Almighty God is the most effective Farmer, Entrepreneur, and Multiplier in the universe. Rather than adding a little extra all the time, His creative power produces multiplier effects on the seeds of your obedience, which often leads to multiplication. He will turn your sown seeds into massive harvests through the power of multiplication. For God, multiplication has never been simply an option. It is a divine principle that infuses the very nature of His life, inherent in His life, and unavoidable wherever there is His life.

As your foundation solidifies, your effort compounds, and you're beginning to look beyond the immediate. This is where strategic planning and scaling come into play. You've proven your concept. Now is the time to expand your reach, optimize your operations, and build a team. The business attracts more customers, not just through direct sales, but through word of mouth, referrals, and reputation. Investments bring in the first returns, and those returns are reinvested, accelerating growth. This is the power of multiplication; where each new success leads to multiple new opportunities. Instead of simply adding, you're now multiplying your efforts. This is where your vision truly starts taking shape, where the seeds you planted blossom. You're not just building a business; you're building a system, a machine capable of generating growth and value.

- Your growing brand doesn't just sell; it attracts
- Strategic partnerships multiply your market presence.
- Smart marketing multiplies your customer base.
- Your investments yield juicy returns.
- Investments don't just return capital; they generate income streams.
- Your well-trained team doesn't just execute tasks; they innovate, they expand, they amplify your individual output.
- A single decision, a single investment, a single partnership produces a ripple effect, amplifying your impact far beyond what you could achieve on your own.

This is the stage where momentum builds, where one success breeds another. This is the stage where business and investing are no longer about working for money, but about making money and influence work for you.

God's system of multiplication defies human logic. Often, what cannot be achieved in a timely fashion through addition, God pulls off by multiplication in an instant. The south-bound voyager says: 'The little I have is not enough to meet my needs, so there is no extra to sow'. But God deals in covenant, and His covenants have standing principles.

Eat your seed and remain at the same level. Keep your seed in perpetuity and it remains the same, loses value, or gets lost. Sow your seed, even if you do so teary-eyed; totally unsure of the outcome. The Multiplier will exceed your expectations.

The Majesty of Exponential Power

In Gen 1:27-29, God gave them seed-trees and asked them to sow and reap fruits. Then, inside the fruits were seeds which, when sown, would produce a greater harvest. Yet, inside those harvests were even more seeds for even more sowing for even more harvests. This is compound interest. This is the way to harness God's amplifying power.

The amplifier effect becomes stimulated when you repeat the process that brought about multiplication in the first place, in which case, you are sowing your already-multiplied seeds. This is simply multiplying what was initially multiplied! This is simply tapping into God's exponential or amplifying power.

Now, let's link your multiplied seed with the Scripture in Psalm 144:13:

> **That our garners may be full, affording all manner of store; that our sheep may bring forth thousands and ten thousands in our streets:** Psalms 144:13 (KJV).

Did you notice the pluralised thousand? Did you spot the pluralised ten thousand also? How often do you see 'ten thousand' pluralised? Do you figure out that this verse is overloaded with unprecedented amplifying power?

On the face value, someone may imagine multiplying ten thousand by two or three, and getting twenty or thirty thousand. But that is only multiplication power. Since that scripture pluralised ten thousand, someone else can choose to envision raising ten thousand to the power of two or three! I hope you can see the difference? One utilises multiplying power while the other harnesses exponential dynamics. The former is like selling your seeds to double or triple the initial capital. But the latter is like sowing your multiplied seeds in two or three iterations to open two or three equally profitable branches of your venture. That is exponential power in full swing.

In investing and business, this is the most powerful stage: where efforts no longer grow in simple increments but explode in leaps and bounds. This is the most breath-taking force of your investment and entrepreneurial rhythm. This is exponential power, the force that turns small businesses into empires and ordinary investors into moguls. This is where true wealth, both financial and personal, is created.

It's not just about accumulating profits, but about building something that lasts, something that has a lasting impact. It's about compounding interest, what some call the eighth wonder of the world. A small investment, given enough time, growing exponentially, becomes far greater than the sum of its parts. The principle applies to your business venture and investment portfolio. Consistent innovation, strategic reinvestment, and a relentless focus on long-term value creation unleash your power of exponential growth.

- A startup that once struggled to gain its first 100 customers suddenly finds itself serving millions.
- An investment portfolio that once added a few dollars each month now compounds at an unstoppable rate.
- A brand that once needed advertising now dominates markets purely through recognition and loyalty.

This is the realm of scalability, automation, and legacy. This is where wealth is no longer measured in numbers alone but in impact, influence, and intergenerational success. You're not just creating wealth; you're creating opportunities, jobs, and a positive ripple effect that extends far beyond your life and lifetime.

In this explosive realm of increase, imagine:

- Your simple seed, sown in tears, erupts into a sprawling, majestic forest, with its roots clawing through continents!
- Your humble book, once captive on silent pages, echoes across continents in different languages!
- Your lone branch births a thriving network.
- Your local label transforms into a world-renowned brand.
- Your product, once meek, now explodes into versions, conquering global markets, and crystalizing into an entire product empire.
- Your service, sharp as a blade, replicates itself with franchises blooming like wildfire, relentless, inevitable!
- Your song explodes into symphonies, igniting a chain of albums that flood through speakers and penetrate millions of waiting souls with its rhythm.
- Your film cracks open and spills sequels, developing into a full-blown series that surges into season after season–unfolding, hungry, infinite!
- Your venture, born in fragile whispers, rises into a multinational powerhouse, swallowing maps and morphing into a global driving force!

This is not mere growth. This is the fever-dream of scale made manifest! This is transformation forged in fury! This is expansion becoming an eruption!

The Vision beyond Today

A business venture and an investment portfolio are not mere tools for financial gain; they are vehicles for transformation. Voyagers who commit to this path experience something beyond wealth. They gain the wisdom of patience, the power of strategy, and the fulfilment of creating something larger than themselves.

To the aspiring entrepreneur, to the steadfast investor, know this:

- In the short-term, every effort counts; addition builds the foundation.
- In the medium term, momentum amplifies; multiplication accelerates progress.
- In the long-term, greatness takes flight: exponential power changes destinies.

Do not be discouraged by the slow start. Do not fear the hurdles along the way. For those who align themselves with the principles that power the forces of addition, multiplication, and exponential growth, success is not a matter of "if" but of "when."

The music of your creation awaits. Conduct it with passion, precision, and an unwavering belief in the power of your dreams.

Build. Invest. Grow. And watch as the seeds you plant today become the forests of tomorrow.